Jagdgeschwader Nr II

Geschwader Berthold

Aviation Elite Units • 19

OSPREY
PUBLISHING

Jagdgeschwader Nr II

Geschwader Berthold

Greg VanWyngarden

Series editor Tony Holmes

Front Cover
Late in the afternoon of 26 September 1918, Ltn Franz Büchner led a flight of eight green-nosed blue Fokker D VIIs on a patrol over Charpentrie, in the Verdun sector. The 20-year-old Büchner was commander of *Jagdstaffel* 13, one of the leading units of *Jagdgeschwader* II, and before the day was out he would set a *Geschwader* record of four confirmed victories to bring his overall total to 36. At about the same time, a flight of four SPAD VIIs from the 94th Aero Squadron left their airfield at 1725 hrs to attack a German balloon. The flight, led by the experienced Lt Alden Sherry, was scheduled to rendezvous with a flight of SPADs from the 27th Aero Squadron, which failed to show up. Worse yet, two of the 94th SPADs dropped out with engine trouble, leaving the rookie pilot Lt Alan Nutt as Sherry's lone companion. The two Americans had just flown over Forges when they unluckily ran into *Jasta* 13. In a letter to Nutt's father, Sherry explained;

'Alan followed me as I crossed the lines north of Verdun and headed towards the balloon. When I was a couple of miles in the German lines, I saw eight Fokkers coming out above us and immediately turned back towards our lines as they dove on us. Five of them attacked me and put my motor out of commission and then followed me to the ground. I crashed in a shell hole a few hundred feet inside our lines. That night I slept in a dugout close by where I fell, and the next morning, on hearing that an American aeroplane had been brought down, I hunted it up and found it was Alan's. The infantrymen told me he put up a magnificent fight with the three aeroplanes attacking him. The third pilot shot him in the chest and head, undoubtedly killing him instantly. He fell near the village of Drillancourt.'

It seems likely that Nutt fell to Büchner, who may have also downed Sherry, although Büchner's fellow *Jasta* 13 pilot Albert Haussmann was also credited with a SPAD on this day. What is certain is that Büchner would be credited with the destruction of four SPADs as part of the grim haul of 14 American aircraft destroyed by the veteran fighter pilots of JG II this day. He flew a D VII emblazoned with his lion emblem and the green and white chequerboard indicative of his Saxon origins. Büchner would survive the war with 40 aircraft to his credit, ranking him as the second-highest-scoring pilot in JG II – the only one to obtain more victories was his old commander Rudolf Berthold.

Although he was no longer with the group, it was the resolute and iron-willed Berthold who had moulded JG II into a crack formation that would earn a fearsome reputation at the expense of the US units in September 1918 (*Cover artwork by Mark Postlethwaite*)

First published in Great Britain in 2005 by Osprey Publishing
1st Floor, Elms Court, Chapel Way, Botley, Oxford, OX2 9LP

ISBN 1 84176 727 1

Edited by Tony Holmes
Page design by Mark Holt
Cover Artwork by Mark Postlethwaite
Aircraft Profiles by Harry Dempsey
Index by Alison Worthington
Origination by Grasmere Digital Imaging, Leeds, UK
Printed in Hong Kong through Bookbuilders

05 06 07 08 09   10 9 8 7 6 5 4 3 2 1

ACKNOWLEDGEMENTS
The author owes a great debt to many people for their help in compiling this work. Special thanks go to Peter M Grosz, Dan-San Abbott, Lance Bronnenkant, Jörn Leckscheid, George H Williams, Paul S Leaman, Stephen Lawson, Dave Roberts, Ray Rimell, Dr Dieter H M Gröschel, H Hugh Wynne, Norman Franks, Frank Olynyk, Frank Bailey, Reinhard Kastner, Volker Haeusler, Uwe Sierts, Charlie Woolley and too many others to name. Alex Imrie provided valuable photos and advice, and his pioneering works on German aviation, and in particular his book *The Fokker Triplane*, were indispensable. Manfred Thiemeyer also generously provided rare photos and priceless information and insights. Rick Duiven's *Jasta* data was extremely valuable, as always. Other unique photographic material and data were kindly provided by Helge K-Werner Dittmann, whose website at www.Flieger-Album.de is highly recommended. Thanks are extended to Terry 'Taz' Phillips and to Wesley Henry, Brett Stolle, Doug Lantry, Jeff Duford and Christina Waszczak at the USAF Museum who went to such effort to provide copies of the Arthur Rahn albums. The staff of the History of Aviation Collection at the University of Texas in Dallas were also extremely helpful. O'Brien Browne provided wonderful translations of German material. The author's many colleagues at *Over the Front* (www.overthefront.com), *Cross and Cockade International* (www.crossandcockade.com) and the Aerodrome Forum (www.theaerodrome.com) were extremely helpful as usual.

CONTENTS

BORN IN BATTLE

Following the success of *Jagdgeschwader* Nr I in 1917 under the command of Manfred von Richthofen, the decision to form two additional *Geschwader* was made by the *Kommandieren General der Luftstreitkräfte (Kogenluft)*, Gen Ernst von Höppner. A *Jagdgeschwader* was a permanent grouping of four *Jagdstaffeln* (*Jasta*) German fighter squadrons with an official strength of 14 aeroplanes. Effectively a fighter wing, a *Geschwader* was under the direct command of the *Armee Oberkommando* or *AOK* (headquarters) of a particular German army. Its purpose was to be rapidly deployable to different areas of the frontline to maintain aerial supremacy by attacking enemy bomber and reconnaissance aircraft in the upper air space.

On 2 February 1918, *Jagdgeschwader* Nr II was formed under the command of the famed Bavarian ace Hptm Adolf Ritter von Tutschek. JG II was composed of *Jagdstaffeln* 12, 13, 15 and 19 in the German 7. *Armee* sector (at the same time JG III was formed from *Jagdstaffeln* 'Boelcke', comprising *Jagdstaffeln* 26, 27 and 36 in the 4. *Armee* sector). These units were intended to reach operational status in time for the massive offensive planned for 21 March. While von Tutschek would lead JG II in its first month, his death on 10 March 1918 was followed by the appointment of the combative and determined Hptm Rudolf Berthold as commander. It was Berthold who would arguably have the greatest impact on the particular character and impressive accomplishments of JG II.

Hptm Adolf Ritter von Tutschek, leader of *Jasta* 12, poses by the wing of his all-black Albatros D III (probably 2274/16) circa May 1917. Von Tutschek, destined to be the first *Kommandeur* of JG II, wears a coveted RFC leather jacket 'liberated' from a British prisoner. Von Tutschek had first flown a black Albatros in *Jasta* Boelcke, and introduced the use of black tails and white spinners for unit insignia to *Jasta* 12. His own D III was apparently entirely black, with national insignia on the wings and tail, backed by white square fields. Note the rack of flare cartridges beside the cockpit

This *Jasta* 12 Albatros D III (thought to be 1960/16) was flown by Ltn Oskar Müller, the technical officer of the *Staffel*. The black/white chevron on the fuselage was Müller's personal marking. The early style of unit marking is displayed – the fuselage and tail was painted black, from the leading edge of the white cross field aft. At this early stage (about April 1917), the white cross fields formed part of the unit's particular decoration (*HAC/UTD*)

Fortunately, historian Hanns Möller chronicled the story of *Jagdgeschwader* II in his book *Kampf und Sieg eines Jagdgeschwaders*, published in 1939 when many veterans of the unit were still alive. Alhough obviously propagandistic, Möller's book remains a valuable source of data and first-hand accounts.

On 2 February 1918, pursuant to the orders of *Kriegsministerium Nr* 452.18.A7L, Royal Prussian *Jagdgeschwader* II was mobilised within the 7. *Armee* sector. Having fully recovered from a wound suffered the previous August, von Tutschek busied himself with the selection of staff for the group and other organisational details. He picked Oblt Heinz Krapfenbauer, whom he had known in his days at Bavarian Fl. Abt. 6, as adjutant for the *Geschwader*. The technical officer for the group would be Ltn Oskar Müller.

On 8 February von Tutschek wrote in his diary, 'Tomorrow or the day after, I wander on down to the 7. *Armee*. The three mechanics, Schuster, Balzer and Bauer, are already underway. We'll see how everything turns out. I am looking forward tremendously to the arrival of my group.' On the 9th he proceeded on to Marle, about 20 km north-east of Laon, 'where I will settle temporarily. I have been unbelievably busy, and in addition there is much work with the *Geschwader*.'

The four component *Staffeln* began assembling in the vicinity of Marle during the first two weeks of February. JG II would begin operations opposite the junction of the British Fifth Army and the French Sixth Army. Thus its opponents would include aircraft of both nations. Von Tutschek's old *Jasta* 12, under the command of Oblt Paul Blumenbach, transferred from Roucourt in the 6. *Armee* to its new airfield at Marle. There it joined *Jasta* 13, commanded by Ltn d R Wolfgang Güttler.

Ltn Hans von Budde commanded *Jasta* 15, located at Autremencourt. *Jagdstaffel* 19, under the command of Ltn Konrad von Bülow-Bothkamp, transferred from St Loup, in the 1. *Armee* sector to Cuirieux on 6

7

February, and about a week later von Bülow was replaced by Ltn d R Walter Göttsch from *Jasta* 8. On the 11th, von Tutschek recorded that there were yet many difficulties to iron out, and he felt the group still lacked adequate aircraft. On the next day:

'I am up to my ears in work trying to get my group organised. I berate, curse, and wander from one high place to another, and am letting my "Blue Max" dangle out more and more as I ramble about in my car on the behalf of my four *Jagdstaffeln*, with good results.'

Jasta 12 moved forward from Marle to Toulis on 13 February, and that same day *Jasta* 13 transferred to Reneuil Ferme. The *Geschwader* headquarters staff was attached to *Jasta* 12 at Toulis, and this unit became the *Stab* (staff) *Staffel* with which the commander lived and flew. Von Tutschek wrote on that day:

'I have a most attractive billet. Three large windows, a comfortable bed, a couch, desk, club chairs and a good heating stove. There are also four electric lights and an electric bell to summon Hans, my orderly. The food is excellent, and I am once again eating with my old *Staffel,* of which Oblt Blumenbach is the leader. He is a marvellous fellow. My mechanics and 25 of my staff are already here. Aside from that there is much work to be done – written and orally.'

On that same 13 February, von Tutschek made JG II's first patrol. He was flying Albatros D V D.2194/17, which was the same aircraft in which he had been shot down in the previous August. Three days later he wrote:

'The new triplanes are to arrive today. Oblt Krapfenbauer is also expected. In short, we'll soon be able to open shop. My *Geschwader* is in fine shape.'

All four *Staffeln* were beginning to re-equip with new Fokker triplanes, but they retained some Albatros and Pfalz fighters. On the 18th von Tutschek test flew a new Dr I, and the next day he wrote, 'This afternoon, my adjutant and I are going to visit the various *Staffeln* of my *Geschwader* in order to get acquainted with all of the fellows.'

JAGDSTAFFEL 12

Von Tutschek was, of course, already quite familiar with *Jasta* 12 as he had commanded the unit for over three months. It was the most successful of the four *Staffeln* at this time. Formed on 6 October 1916, it had been built on the personnel of *Fokkerstaffel West*, which had been based at Paux-Fé airfield in the 7. *Armee*. The first *Staffelführer* was Hptm Paul von Osterroht, and the unit was operating from Riencourt in the 1. *Armee* by 4 November. Initially equipped with mediocre Fokker D I biplanes, *Jasta* 12 suffered its first casualties within two weeks, but gained its initial confirmed success with an FE 2 downed on 4 December.

By the end of March 1917 the *Staffel* was flying Albatros fighters, and had achieved ten victories for the loss of two pilots killed and three wounded. Uffz Reinhold Jörke, a relative newcomer who would continue scoring through the formation of JG II, claimed the unit's tenth confirmed victory on 24 March.

Jasta 12 really came into its own in 'Bloody April' of 1917, during the Battle of Arras. *Jasta* 12 was credited with destroying 23 aircraft of the Royal Flying Corps, making it one of the higher-scoring *Staffeln* on the British front. 23 April was especially eventful for the unit, as it gained four

ADOLF VON TUTSCHEK

Adolf Ritter von Tutschek was born into a military family on 16 May 1891 in Ingolstadt, Bavaria. He graduated from the Royal Bavarian Cadet School and began his military service in the 3rd *Bayerischen Infanterie-Regt* in 1910. Von Tutschek was commissioned shortly before the war started. In *Infanterie-Regt* Nr 40 he saw considerable action on the Western Front, before being transferred east in 1915. On 25 July he volunteered to lead his unit in an attack on a vital Russian position south of Petrilow. Von Tutschek and his men took the objective and held it against counter-attack for 17 days – a feat which earned him the Knight's Cross of the Bavarian Max-Joseph Order. He then returned to France and suffered his second wound of the war at Verdun.

After recovering, von Tutschek was accepted for pilot training and was posted to Bavarian F. Fl. Abt. 6 in October 1916. His sterling service flying two-seaters earned him the Bavarian Military Merit Order 4th Class with Crown and Swords on 17 January, and eight days later he happily reported to *Jasta* Boelcke to take up his career as a fighter pilot. In this elite unit von Tutschek flew alongside such present and future luminaries as Richthofen, Voss, Bernert and Boehme. After two unconfirmed claims, he forced down a DH 2 for his first official victory on 6 March, followed by a Nieuport on the 31st. A third victory convinced his superiors that he had the command and flying experience to lead his own *Staffel,* and on 28 April 1917 he was named commander of *Jasta* 12.

Von Tutschek took his new post reluctantly, and felt a bit of a 'foreigner' amidst the Prussians of *Jasta* 12. He soon settled in, however, and under the guidance of the wiry Bavarian, *Jasta* 12 earned a reputation as a crack unit. On 23 May, with his score at ten, he exchanged his black Albatros D III for a new D V, which he took for a test flight. Encountering a flight of Sopwiths, he attacked, but his synchronisation gear failed and he barely survived when he shot off his own propeller. Despite this setback, von Von Tutschek continued to score, and on 11 July he achieved his 12th and 13th victories, and was honoured with the 'Hohenzollern'. By 3 August his tally stood at 21, and he received his 'Blue Max', but was wounded eight days later.

While recovering, von Tutschek was promoted to hauptmann on 6 December. During his convalescence he wrote his memoirs – his publisher suggested the title 'The Black Air Fighter', which he rejected as 'too Richthofenish', and went instead with *Sturme und Luftsiege* (*Attack and Air Victories*). On 1 February 1918 he was given leadership of the new JG II. As *Geschwader Kommandeur*, he despatched four more enemies to bring his total to 27 before he was killed in action on 15 March flying his Dr I 404/17.

Hptm Adolf Ritter von Tutschek displays his *Pour le Mérite* and other decorations in this popular Sanke postcard image. Von Tutschek's firm hand and charismatic leadership was exactly what was needed to start JG II off on the right foot

confirmed victories (and three unconfirmed), but von Osterroht was killed in Albatros D III D.1958/16 after downing his seventh opponent. His place as *Staffelführer* was soon filled very capably by Oblt von Tutschek, a veteran of *Jasta* Boelcke with three confirmed claims. Arriving on 30 April, he made an impressive start at his new command that very afternoon. FE 2b aircraft from No 57 Sqn raided the field at Epinoy, and von Tutschek led his pilots into the air and shot down one of the 'Fees' in short order.

In May the *Staffel* added 16 more claims, and von Tutschek could write on the 10th, 'My *Staffel* and I are in top shape in every respect.' Ten more aircraft fell to the unit in June, one of which was the first victory of 29-year-old Ltn d R Hermann Becker, a veteran two-seater pilot who had just joined the *Jasta* in mid-May. He accounted for a Sopwith Pup on 6 June, but was severely wounded ten days later. Becker would eventually return to the *Jasta*, and great success. After a dry spell in June, von Tutschek went on a veritable rampage the next month. He was responsible for 11 of the 15 victories *Jasta* 12 achieved in July, bringing the unit's total to an impressive 74.

However, after scoring a 'double' over Bristol Fighters on 11 August, von Tutschek was himself shot down by British ace C D Booker of 8 Naval Squadron. Severely wounded in the right shoulder, the Bavarian managed to land safely, but was out of action for six months. Acting command of *Jasta* 12 was briefly held by Ltn von Nostitz, then the unit was taken over by Ltn d R Viktor Schobinger, a Württemberger who had seen only three weeks of service in *Jasta* 12. He would become an eight-victory ace and highly proficient combat leader. In three months under Schobinger, *Jasta* 12 Albatros pilots destroyed 22 British aircraft without suffering a single casualty.

Vfw Reinhold Jörke had brought his personal tally to eight by 17 September – a month that also provided another youngster with his first step on the climb to the *Pour le Mérite*. Nineteen-year-old Uffz Ulrich Neckel had only arrived at the *Staffel* on 8 September, but 13 days later he succeeded in claiming a 'Sopwith' for his initial victory. By November Neckel's score had already reached three, as had Becker's. More importantly, the *Staffel* had also celebrated its 100th victory on the last day of October. Schobinger's run of success came to an end on 15 November when he was seriously wounded in the right foot and left *Jasta* 12.

Again, von Nostitz took acting command, but in December Prussian ex-field artillery officer Oblt Paul Blumenbach arrived from *Jasta* 13 to lead the *Staffel*. In the first six weeks of 1918 only four victories were achieved for the loss of one pilot killed and another taken PoW. Nonetheless, at the time of von Tutschek's return to form JG II, *Jasta* 12 was still one of the best in the German Army, with 104 victories and a talented core of performers like Blumenbach, Neckel, Becker and Jörke.

JAGDSTAFFEL 13

Jasta 13 was officially formed in *Armee Detachment 'Strantz'* area from Fokker pilots in *Eindecker-Staffel* I attached to Fl. Abt. 19 and 8, and other single-seater pilots from *Eindecker-Staffel* II of Fl. Abt. 3b and 70. Although the official establishment date is listed as 28 September 1916, it was almost a month before the *Jasta* reached operational status at Mars la Tour. Its first commander was Oblt Erhardt Egerer. Operating on the French front, *Jasta* 13 finally achieved its first success on 22 January 1917 when a Caudron fell to the guns of Oblt Eduard Dostler, a Bavarian who had scored his initial two victories as a two-seater pilot in *Kampfstaffel* 36. Dostler's rise to prominence would take place elsewhere, as he was transferred to take command of *Jasta* 34 on 20 February.

The airmen of *Jasta* 13 achieved somewhat mediocre results in the first half of 1917, attaining seven confirmed claims over Caudrons and

Leutnant Pippart

Ltn d L Hans Martin Pippart joined Jasta 13 in December 1917, and would become one of the true superstars of JG II. At 29 years of age, the native of Mannheim was older and far more experienced than many of his fellow pilots. Together with Heinrich Noll, he had established the firm of Pippart und Noll in 1913 to design and construct *Eindecker* aircraft. From the onset of the war, Pippart served as both an instructor and frontline pilot, and would eventually rise to the command of Jasta 19

Farmans for the loss of one pilot killed and another injured. Two SPADs were credited in August, plus a two-seater the following month. September also saw the arrival of a future highly decorated ace whose name is closely linked with the story of *Jagdstaffel* 13 – Ltn Franz Büchner, a 19-year-old Saxon who had transferred in from *Jasta* 9 with one victory awaiting confirmation.

In October young Büchner claimed a SPAD to contribute to a total of four in that month for the *Staffel*. One of these fell on the 30th to Ltn d R Wolfgang Güttler, who had arrived only the previous day to take command of the unit. The 24-year-old Güttler had served as a two-seater pilot in Fl. Abt. 72 on the Eastern Front in 1916, and following fighter training had attained his first four triumphs in *Jasta* 24. The SPAD he downed on 30 October was therefore his fifth victory, and he added another on 2 December.

Eleven days later Güttler welcomed another veteran airman to the *Staffel*, Ltn d L Hans Pippart. The 29-year-old Pippart was a native of Mannheim, in Baden. He was also a pre-war pilot, having designed and flown his own monoplane and set an endurance record in 1913. He had then flown both two-seaters and fighters in Fl. Abt. A 220 on the Galician Front. Despite relatively little enemy aerial activity there, Pippart had achieved six victories (including three balloons) and received several high awards from Prussia and Baden. He did not immediately add to his tally in December or January, months in which *Jasta* 13 achieved six victories for the loss of two pilots killed. At its incorporation into JG II, *Jagdstaffel* 13 had 22 victories and a promising future with stalwarts like Pippart and Büchner in its ranks.

JAGDSTAFFEL 15

Jasta 15 was destined to successfully claim over 150 victories in its varied career. In late September/early October 1916, the fighter detachment known as *Kampfeinsitzer Kommando (KEK) Habsheim*, in the *Armee Detachment* 'B' sector, began its transformation into a permanent *Jagdstaffel*.

The first commander was Oblt Kropp, and the unit was considered operational by 9 October. One of the former *KEK Habsheim* pilots was a young Vfw Ernst Udet, who already had one victory. He scored his second on 12 October – the day the *Staffel* formed part of the effort to intercept a massive Anglo-French raid on the Mauser Factory at Oberndorf. Three bombers fell to Fokker D IIs flown by *Jasta* 15 pilots on the 12th. In November, Oblt Max Reinhold transferred from *Jasta* 6 to take over leadership of the unit, which continued to score sporadically against Caudrons and Nieuports for the next six months.

In early March 1917 the *Staffel* transferred to Sissone in the 7. *Armee*, and by 24 April ten aircraft were credited to the unit (four by Udet), now equipped with Albatros D IIIs. However, two days later the unit lost its leader when Reinhold fell as its second fatal casualty.

The *Staffel* was fortunate in his successor. Ltn d R Heinrich Gontermann was a Westphalian veteran of *Jasta* 5 with 17 victories. Only 21, Gontermann brought a reputation as a 'balloon buster', and a mature leadership style to *Jasta* 15. He had been one of the leading lights of 'Bloody April', with six balloons and five aircraft downed in three weeks.

An interesting mixed bag of Albatros and Pfalz types is seen in this line-up of *Jasta* 15 fighters, photographed before the formation of JG II, perhaps in the autumn of 1917. Third from the front is the Pfalz D III flown by Ltn Claus von Waldow, decorated with his personal stylised 'N' emblem within a rectangular frame. The seventh aircraft (an Albatros D V) may have been flown by Ltn d R Heinrich Arntzen, as it seems to bear his typical black/white quartering. Arntzen would attain two victories in *Jasta* 15, and then bring his tally to 11 in *Jasta* 50. Next in line is another Pfalz D III, which is possibly one of Hans Müller's aeroplanes. The Albatros D V in the foreground with the white 'death's head' marking should not be taken for the machine of Georg von Hantelmann, for he was not in *Jasta* 15 at this time

Ltn d R Kurt Monnington is seen in his highly decorated Albatros D V of *Jasta* 15, circa autumn 1917. This machine bore a raggedly applied camouflage pattern on its fuselage, with a personal marking of a detailed 'death's head' on a white band on the fuselage. Monnington would score no victories in *Jasta* 15, and only briefly served in JG II, but after transferring to *Jasta* 18 in the 'Berthold Swap' on 20 March 1918, he would achieve eight victories (*via U Sierts*)

In early May *Jasta* 15 was transferred to Boncourt. In that month Gontermann added four more aircraft, and Udet wounded French ace Alfred Heurtaux of *Escadrille* SPA3 on the 5th. *Jasta* 15 was indeed situated opposite the famous *Cigogne* group at this time, and five days after Udet's victory, Gontermann shot down the four-victory SPA3 pilot Adj Sanglier. Gontermann's 'Blue Max' came four days after on 14 May.

Things did not always go the Germans' way, however, as four *Jasta* 15 pilots were killed in 11 days at the end of May/early June. Among the pilots who transferred into the unit in June and July were future aces Ltn d L Karl Albert Mendel (eight victories), Ltn d R Kurt Monnington (eight) and Ltn d R Hans Müller (13). They were slow starters, however, and none of them would play much of a role in JG II for reasons that will become evident.

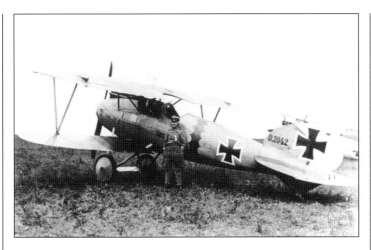

Albatros D V 2042/17 of *Jasta* 15 forms a superb backdrop for Vfw Albert Haussmann in 1917. Haussmann's D V bore his personal insignia of an 'engrailed' fuselage band, but *Jasta* 15 aircraft displayed no unit markings at this time under Heinrich Gontermann's command. The apparent dark 'pennant' trailing back from the cockpit is actually evidence that the factory-installed headrest has been removed from this D V. Haussmann had attained his first victories in *Jasta* 23, then transferred to *Jasta* 15 in June 1917. A year later he was flying the Fokker D VII in *Jasta* 13, and was one of the real standouts of JG II (*HAC/UTD*)

Udet transferred out to *Jasta* 37 on 26 July, and Gontermann was left to score all of the unit's triumphs in mid-summer 1917. He continued his vendetta against French balloons, adding six 'gasbags' and two aeroplanes by 9 August for a total of 28. Another balloon fell to *Jasta* 15 on 13 August, but this one was credited to up-and-coming Vfw Albert Haussmann, an ex-*Jasta* 23 pilot who also claimed a Nieuport that day.

Haussmann had downed his first victim as a pilot in *Kampfstaffel* 26 of KG 5 in October 1916, then three more with *Jasta* 23 before being transferred to *Jasta* 15 in June. He was destined for even greater achievements in JG II. For the rest of August and September, Gontermann's success persisted. On 2 October he downed a SPAD to bring his final score to 17 balloons and 22 aeroplanes destroyed.

Jasta 15 had transferred from Boncourt to La Neuville on 20 August, and it was there that tragedy struck on 30 October. Gontermann had received one of the first Fokker triplanes to be sent to the 7. *Armee*, and he was delighted with his Dr I, 115/17. During a test flight, however, the upper wing suffered structural failure and Gontermann was fatally injured in the crash. He died in the field hospital at Marle, and the Dr I was temporarily grounded.

Gontermann's close friend Ltn Hans Hermann von Budde assumed command of *Jasta* 15, but few additional successes would come the unit's way before its inclusion in *Jagdgeschwader* II. Only two victories were attained in January 1918, by the promising Hans Müller. However, with approximately 47 victories and a proud lineage, the pilots of *Jasta* 15 were ready to perform their duties as a vital component of JG II.

JAGDSTAFFEL 19

The story of the early history and origins of Royal Prussian *Jasta* 19 is a bit more murky than that of the other JG II components. The formation date is recorded as 25 October 1916 at *Armee Flug Park* 1 in the 1. *Armee.* The unit's first commander was the Bavarian Oblt Franz Walz, who had already scored six victories in *Kagohl* I and received the Knight's Cross with Swords of the Royal Hohenzollern House Order (known simply as 'the Hohenzollern'). His time at *Jasta* 19 was brief, as he left to command *Jasta* 2 on 28 November. Walz's place was taken by Saxon Oblt Erich Hahn, a former pilot with Fl. Abt. 23 and Fl. Abt. A 221. Hahn had served

Ltn d R Hans Müller of *Jasta* 15 downed his first opponent on 9 January 1918, followed by another French two-seater 20 days later. After being transferred to *Jasta* 18 in the great switch in March, he would go on to achieve 13 victories, most of them while flying a red and white Fokker D VII in the summer. He is seen here with his *Jasta* 15 Albatros D III (OAW), which bore his usual band of diagonal black and white stripes and similar wheel décor (*via U Sierts*)

It was the frequent custom in *Jasta* 19 to mark the Albatros fighters of the unit with their pilot's initials in stylised black characters with white shading. Albatros D II 1737/16 is seen on the *Jasta* 19 airfield, displaying a personal 'G' insignia. Close examination of the photo shows that this 'G' may have been applied over a previous marking ('W'?) which had been removed. At any rate, 1737/16 may have been flown by Ltn d R Gerlt, who served in *Jasta* 19 both in 1917 and 1918. He was wounded on 4 May 1917, and served as acting commander of the unit twice in the summer of 1918 (*Arthur Rahn collection, United States Air Force Museum*)

Ltn d R Walter Böning was a highly decorated pilot from Oldenburg who drew the first blood for *Jasta* 19 by downing a French pusher on 6 April 1917. He claimed another aircraft on the 29th and one of the five balloons *Jasta* 19 burned on the 30th. Böning later took over command of *Jasta* 76b. He is seen here posing with his Albatros D V 2091/17. While previously identified as a *Jasta* 76b aircraft, it is now clear that this D V was actually Böning's machine in *Jasta* 19, and was photographed at St Loup. The wings and tailplane were camouflaged in green and mauve, and the rudder may have been dark camouflage green as well. Böning had his 'B' insignia applied on a black-bordered white band, and the nose is decorated too. As leader of *Jasta* 76b, he would bring his score to 17 before being wounded on 31 May 1918 (*HAC/UTD*)

as a fighter pilot in *Jasta* 1, and scored his first allowed claim on 10 November 1916.

The *Jasta* 19 pilots did not even start to receive their first Albatros D IIs until December 1916, but by the beginning of 1917 they were flying sorties from their base at Saarburg, near Bühl, in the *Armee Detachment* 'A' sector. The unit achieved little in its first months. On 30 January 1917, Ltn d R Reinhold Oertelt was injured in a crash, and the same fate befell the East Prussian pilot Vfw Arthur Rahn on 5 February. After a short time in hospital with a broken nose, Rahn returned to go on to greater things.

The unit moved to Thour, north of Reims, on 19 March. *Jasta* 19 finally made its first mark on 6 April when Ltn d R Walter Böning sent a Caudron G 4 of *Escadrille* C227 down for the first of his eventual 17 victories. Two days later Hahn contributed another Caudron for the second success for himself and his *Staffel*. The pilots now began to make up for lost time, their best day coming on the last day of 'Bloody April'. Hahn and Rahn were both credited with the destruction of two French balloons, and Böning flamed another for a total of five for the day.

Mixed fortunes returned to the *Jasta* for the next four months. In May two pilots were badly wounded in exchange for four confirmed claims,

including the third for Rahn. 12 May saw the all-important first victory for Ltn d R Wilhelm Leusch as he downed a SPAD fighter south of Berry au Bac. A native of Dusseldorf, Leusch was a veteran of service with F. Fl. Abt. 19, and had transferred from *Jasta* 13 in April (he would become a stalwart member of *Jasta* 19, and its last commander). In June the *Jasta* moved from St Fergeux to St Loup airfield in the 1. *Armee*. On 7 July, Oertelt was killed by the French ace Guynemer, but the following month saw three *Staffel* victories without a loss.

On 3 September, French balloons were burned by NCO pilots Martin Mallmann and Albert Tybelsky – the first confirmed claims for both. The following day Erich Hahn was killed in combat with ace Lt George Madon of N38 over the Champagne. In the following three weeks, Mallmann crashed a Caudron and Böning destroyed two Nieuports to bring the *Staffel* total to 24, and Ltn d R Ernst Hess arrived from *Jasta* 28 on 18 September to replace the fallen Hahn. Hess was a proven *Jagdflieger* with 14 confirmed victims to his name, and he claimed a further three French aircraft in October.

That month also saw the departure of Arthur Rahn to *Jasta* 18, but he would eventually return to his old *Staffel* six months later. Hess was killed

Although slightly blurred, this photo reveals the Albatros D V fighters of *Jasta* 19 at St Loup airfield in the late summer of 1917. First in line is D V 2111/17, emblazoned with an 'M' insignia and probably flown by Vfw Martin Mallmann, who attained three victories before being killed on 19 January 1918. The second D V is 2014/17, marked 'T' and most likely flown by Uffz Albert Tybelsky, a long-serving pilot of the unit. All of the aircraft appear to have fairly dark rudders, which were probably painted in camouflage olive green. Note that some aircraft were marked with coloured fuselage bands instead of initials for personal emblems (*HAC/UTD*)

Ltn d R Franz Dotzel, who served in *Jasta* 19 from October 1916 to 19 June 1917, strikes a confident pose with an Albatros D III bearing his 'Do' insignia in characteristic *Staffel* style. The addition of the 'o' helped distinguish Dotzel's aircraft from that of Ltn Walter Dingel, who used 'Di' on his machine. Note the rack of flare cartridges mounted beside the cockpit. Dotzel served in several different units, and is thought to have been on the strength of *Jasta* 15 in the summer of 1918 (*P M Grosz*)

in Albatros D Va 5347/17 two days before Christmas 1917, and the *Jasta* was again in need of a *Staffelführer*.

By 4 January 1918, Ltn Conrad von Bülow-Bothkamp had been appointed the leader of *Jasta* 19. One of the three famous flying von Bülow-Bothkamp brothers, he brought down a French Sopwith 1¹/₂ Strutter behind German lines on 3 February, but this would be the only successful claim made by *Jasta* 19 under his command. Just after the formation of JG II, Conrad was removed from active duty by Imperial order in response to the death of his famous sibling Walter in January.

The next commander of *Jasta* 19 was Ltn d R Walter Göttsch, who proved to be another fortuitous choice. The 21-year-old Göttsch was a 17-victory veteran of *Jasta* 8 who had also flown in Fl. Abt. 33. He seems to have conducted an almost private war with the RFC's No 20 Sqn, having shot down seven of its aircraft in 1917, and in return being twice slightly wounded by the unit's crews. Göttsch had only recently returned from hospital before taking over his new unit. With 30 victories on the *Staffel* list, the pilots of *Jasta* 19 looked forward to increased success under their new commander, and with the new Fokker triplanes.

INTO COMBAT

Even before von Tutschek made his 'tour' of the four *Staffeln* to meet the men of his new command, *Jagdgeschwader* II had already drawn its first blood. *Jasta* 13 scored the initial victory for JG II on 17 February, when Oblt Alex Thomas brought down a balloon north-east of La Fére. Two days later the same unit's commander, Ltn Güttler, set a Bréguet 14B2 two-seater aflame over Guise for his eighth victim.

However, *Jasta* 13 also suffered the distinction of sustaining the first *Geschwader* casualties on 20 February. After his successful combat the day before, Güttler had been forced to leave his Fokker Dr I on the airfield of *Jasta* 24 at Guise. On the 20th, he and Vfw Paul Hiob took off in a Halberstadt CL II to retrieve the triplane. For some unknown reason, at about 100 metres the two-seater nosed over and crashed just south-east of Renieul Ferme, and both airmen were killed. Güttler's replacement was Oblt Thomas, aptly selected from the *Staffel* ranks.

A youthful-looking Arthur Rahn poses proudly with his pilot's badge and Iron Cross. Rahn was one of the first members of *Jasta* 19, and he achieved the dubious distinction of being the unit's second casualty when he crashed from 75 metres after taking off from Bühl airfield on 5 February 1917. He joined his *Staffel* mate Reinhold Oertelt in the hospital with a broken nose. He was soon back in action though, and participated in his unit's destruction of five balloons on 30 May. In October 1917 he flew in *Jasta* 18 under Berthold, then briefly served in *Jasta* 15, before returning to *Jasta* 19 in March 1918 (*Arthur Rahn collection, United States Air Force Museum*)

Fokker Dr I 218/17 of *Jasta* 15 displays the white cowling characteristic of all JG II triplanes in March 1918 – the first example of a true *Jagdgeschwader* marking. Ltn Bergner shows off the cumbersome *Fliegerkombination* flying kit, tucked into thigh boots, which was standard issue for German airmen. The information board in the background indicates that one aircraft is ready for flight (*Start* being an abbreviation for *Startklar*), with three others being in reserve, or perhaps unserviceable at this time. Bergner was one of the *Jasta* 15 pilots switched en masse with *Jasta* 18 in March, and he went on to fly Fokker D VIIs in the summer (*via P S Leaman*)

Soon after the formation of JG II, a mechanic stands ready to swing the prop on Adolf von Tutschek's Dr I 404/17 at Toulis. Another crewman prepares to hold down the tail as soon as the engine starts, while von Tutschek's chief mechanic Uffz Balzer stands by the cockpit. At this time the *Jasta* 12 unit marking of a white cowling has been effected, but the black tail colouration has been applied only to the tailplane and rear fuselage. All cross-fields and the rudder remain white in this photogaph, but later they would be reduced with black paint to produce the regulation white border around the crosses. Note the leader's streamer trailing from the lower wing and the works number 1988 on both interplane struts. A Morell airspeed indicator is mounted on the port strut. Just visible is the white cloth von Tutschek used for wiping his goggles, tucked under his shoulder harness

Six Fokker triplanes and one Albatros D V of *Jasta* 13 display their white tail unit markings at Reneuil Ferme airfield, in the 7. *Armee*. Very soon they would transfer to Guise, in the 18. *Armee*, in order to participate in the *Kaiserschlacht*. Each Dr I was marked with a white tail and cowling, with personal insignia painted between the fuselage cross and the pilot's seat, The solitary Albatros has a white spinner. The third machine from the right is the triplane of Hans Pippart, identified by his white wavy line emblem (*HAC/UTD*)

Jastas 12 and 13 were both in action on the afternoon of 21 February. Reinhold Jörke (now with *Jasta* 13) entered the ranks of the ten-victory *Kanonen* with an SE 5 downed near Reneuil-Ferme, and his *Staffel* mate Hans Pippart put his Eastern Front experience to use by flaming a British balloon for his seventh victim. The next day von Tutschek forced a two-seater down from 3500 metres to 800 metres over Allied territory, but he had to let it go when his guns jammed. Nonetheless, he was ecstatic over the manoeuvrability of his Fokker Dr I, reporting it was 'a tremendous machine (that) climbs terrifically'.

On 24 February, von Tutschek's faith in his triplane was tested to the extreme. He was out on a Sunday joy ride, but could not resist the temptation of recklessly tackling a group of what he said were 16 SE 5 fighters being shelled by flak over the German lines. He attacked the last one in the formation:

'I aim and fire and think he will go down, but the opposite is the case. To my most unpleasant surprise, my friend banks toward me, shooting. And with him are all 16 SEs. I bank, loop and shoot, trying not to offer the

Fokker Dr I 167/17 of *Jasta* 19 was also marked with an individual yellow numeral, in this case a '3' – the chalk outline used by the *Staffel* painter is clearly discernible. This view provides a fine look at the diagonal black and yellow bands on the tailplane and elevators that made up the unit marking of this *Staffel* at this time. The white cross fields on the upper wing have been reduced with solid olive paint, and this aircraft shows a white cowling in common with other triplanes of JG II. *Staffelführer* Göttsch would soon replace the yellow numerals with white fuselage markings, and also order the fuselage crosses over-painted with streaky camouflage as a further unit identification, and to permit fuller application of individual markings (*P M Grosz*)

One of a series of photos taken of von Tutschek, now JG II commander, and his *Stab Staffel* of *Jasta* 12 shows them at their *Kasino* in Toulis in March 1918. Starting at the top of the steps at left, they are Vfw Ulrich Neckel, Ltn Bock, Ltn d R Hermann Becker (with his dachshund on his left arm), Ltn d R Oskar Müller, Ltn d R Hoffmann, Ltn Staats (half hidden), Oblt Paul Blumenbach (CO), Hptm von Tutschek, Ltn Koch and Oblt a D Krapfenbauer. This photo captured one 'Blue Max' holder (von Tutschek), future winner Neckel (though at this time he had 'only' six victories and was still an NCO) and Becker, who had six of his eventual 23 claims at this time, and who would just miss out on his own *Pour le Mérite*

attacking aircraft a steady target. I go down toward the woods of Crepy. In an easterly direction, in a widening distance behind me, is the yelping pack of hounds. I am now 100 metres above the ground. I look up and am astonished – 12 are tumbling down toward me to partly cut off my path. I pour on the gas and go down to ten metres above the dark woods. Even here, five or six enemy single-seaters follow me. I can't land. There is nothing left to do but take on the SE 5s in an air combat at ten metres altitude, until I or the others run out of gas, or other German aircraft come to my aid, or I receive the fatal shot.

'On top of that, both of my guns, which have delivered 600 rounds smoothly, were now jammed. Rat-tat-tat comes from above and behind. I bank so that the wing almost scrapes the ground and race toward him. In the same instant, more fire from behind and to the side. One Englishman races past under me and the other above me. The wood splinters fly in my face, and the spar above me is splintered and the rudder bar under my foot is hit. Near the ground, I pull up with the motor racing and sit behind the attacker. Thank God my left machine gun is working again.

Victor and vanquished. Von Tutschek poses with SPAD XIII B6732 of No 23 Sqn's 2Lt Doyle, which he shot down on 26 February for his first claim as JG II commander. The Bavarian ace wrote that he fired 50 rounds at the SPAD, holing the fuel tank, and the aircraft came down, 'in good shape near Athies, two km north-east of Laon. Now home and then by auto back to the almost untouched machine. Only the wing, gas tank and the propeller show hits. Then to my Irish Lt Doyle, who seems happy to have gotten off with a grazing shot to the little toe.' Doyle's SPAD was taken to the JG II airfield at Toulis and became a liberally photographed trophy. In the background is von Tutschek's Dr I 404/17, now showing its final display of *Jasta* 12 unit markings

'The gas tank of my opponent is shot through, and with a long white gas vapour trailing, he seeks to escape. I can't fight him down, as already a new one is on my back. After we have amused ourselves in this manner for 15 minutes, the remaining four enemy fighters give up their efforts to shoot me down.'

Von Tutschek arrived safely back at Toulis, having gained 'a deep affection for my Fokker Dr I'.

Jasta 12 was back in combat on an eventful 26 February when von Tutschek forced down the SPAD of 2Lt D C Doyle of No 23 Sqn, who was taken prisoner at Athies, near Laon. Ulrich Neckel achieved his fifth that day by bringing down the SE 5 of No 24 Sqn's 2Lt C H Crosbee, who was also taken PoW. However, No 24 Sqn achieved a measure of retaliation when 2Lt A K Cowper shot down Pfalz D III 4184/17, piloted by Vfw Hegeler of *Jasta* 15, who was captured in turn.

26 February also saw *Jasta* 19 move from Cuirieux to join *Jasta* 12 at Toulis.

On 26 February 1918, Vfw Hegeler of *Jasta* 15 became the first member of JG II to be taken prisoner when his Pfalz D III 4184/17 was shot down by 2Lt Cowper of No 24 Sqn, coming down near Bonneuil. Hegeler had arrived at *Jasta* 15 from *Jasta* 24 only nine days before. His Pfalz became the subject of technical scrutiny (it was given the captured aircraft number G 141), and an article in *Flight* magazine. The pilot's personal emblem was the black sloping band on the fuselage, with ovals 'cut out'

The next day *Jasta* 12 leader Oblt Blumenbach, in company with von Tutschek, downed a 'SPAD two-seater' for his first success. The final day of February was also a full one for *Jasta* 12, as Becker, Koch and Neckel all claimed SE 5 victories (one of them was flown by 2Lt E O Krohn of No 84 Sqn, who was killed in action). Von Tutschek and Blumenbach survived a collision between their two Dr Is, both pilots being able to gently nurse their damaged triplanes down to safe landings.

On 1 March, to 'calm his nerves', von Tutschek flew his repaired Dr I 404/17 out on another patrol with Blumenbach. Von Tutschek attacked a French balloon near Terny. 'After ten shots, the balloon, at an altitude of 3000 metres, burned. A big black box (camera) with a red parachute went over, followed by two white parachutes of the observers. My 25th victory.' The day's success was marred by the loss of Flg Gustav Koriath of *Jasta* 19, who was killed in a crash at St Loup.

The clear skies of 6 March brought a day of intense action for the *Geschwader*. Von Tutschek led a group of three Dr Is and four Albatros in an attack on seven SE 5s from No 24 Sqn, and the *Kommandeur* was once again successful in capturing an enemy machine and pilot (the SE flown by 2Lt A P C Wigan). However, the Albatros D V of Ltn Hans Staats collided with the SE 5 flown by Lt D M Clements of No 24 Sqn and both pilots died (Clements was apparently credited to Becker). Pippart of *Jasta* 13 and Rudolf Rienau of *Jasta* 19 also achieved victories this day, the first of six for Rienau.

Jasta 19's commander Walter Göttsch attacked an unusual target on the 7th – a *German* balloon. It had broken loose from its moorings and was destroyed by Göttsch before it could drift into Allied hands.

Ltn d R Walter Göttsch was brought to JG II from *Jasta* 8 on 14 February 1918 to take over *Jasta* 19. He is seen shortly after this in Fokker Dr I 202/17, which had been despatched from Schwerin on 24 January. His personal marking consisted of a yellow '2' on the sides and top of the fuselage. This emblem was first sketched in chalk outline, the vestiges of which are still visible. The serial number on the lower fuselage was obscured by the large '2' marking, and was thus re-painted in yellow beneath the tailplane (*courtesy M Thiemeyer*)

On 9 March, Ltn Robert Hildebrandt of *Jasta* 13 achieved his first of six victories, and it was an unusual one. Capt James Miller, commander of the new American 95th Aero Squadron (still in the process of forming up at Villeneuve), was invited to go on an ill-advised patrol over the lines with Majs Davenport Johnson and Millard Harmon in some SPADs borrowed from a French *Escadrille*. Harmon dropped out of the flight with engine trouble, but Miller and Johnson pressed on. They encountered several *Jasta* 13 fighters and attacked, but Johnson had to leave the fight with jammed guns. Hildebrandt turned the tables on Miller and fired several long bursts. The 95th lost its first CO as Miller fell south-west of Laon. JG II would claim several more members of the 95th Aero Squadron, including its very last victim of the war.

Von Tutschek attained his 27th victory on 10 March when he downed the SPAD flown by Adj Vallod of SPA86, who was killed:

'On the second patrol with Oblt Blumenbach and Ltn Hoffmann, and flying Fokker Dr I 404/17, we flew under five SPADs at 3000 metres, and they came down on us. I got behind the leader, who after 50 rounds at close range nosed over on fire. It went straight down just north-west of Fort Malmaison, near Chavigon, and crashed in a French trench, where it burned bright and red.'

Von Tutschek and his *Geschwader* were apparently hitting their stride, with *Jasta* 12 responsible for ten of the 18 victories posted by JG II thus far. The pilots and staff were no doubt anticipating the imminent offensive which, it was hoped, would finally win the war for Germany. In response to the news of the treaty with the Soviets, and the coming assault in France, von Tutschek had written on 7 March, 'Our good sword has

Ltn Claus von Waldow was posted to *Jasta* 15 in July 1917, and was still with the unit in March 1918 when his Dr I 412/17 was photographed at Autremencourt, near Marle. He used a stylised 'N' as his personal insignia on more than one aircraft, and it is seen here in white against the dark streaky camouflage of the fuselage. The significance of this letter is unknown but it likely referred to a lady friend. Von Waldow's guns are fitted with auxiliary centrally mounted sights. Von Waldow was also one of those pilots transferred to *Jasta* 18 on 20 March 1918 (*HAC/UTD*)

effected order in Russia. We'll see when the situation in the west begins to click. We are all excited about it.' The very next day he flew to Guise, in the 18. *Armee* sector, to plan the imminent move to that airfield to participate in the offensive.

THE *KOMMANDEUR* FALLS

The most massive German push of the Great War was now in final preparation. The initial phase was code named Operation *Michael*, but its planner, *General der Infanterie* Erich Ludendorff, gave it the simple title of *Kaiserschlacht* – the Emperor's Battle. The collapse of Russia had released thousands of German troops to bolster the forces on the Western Front, and the offensive was designed to achieve a decisive result before American manpower and industrial strength could be brought to bear. Three German armies (the 2., 17. and 18.) would attack the British Fifth and Sixth Armies along the line from Arras to La Fére in an attempt to break through in the direction of Amiens.

For this titanic effort, the three attacking armies were allocated 35 *Jadgstaffeln,* including one *Jagdgeschwader* for each army. The opening day was scheduled for 21 March (*Der Tag*), and it was thus that von Tutschek was preparing to move his *Geschwader* to the 18. *Armee* and lead it in Germany's most momentous battle to date. Fate intervened, however.

On 15 March 1918 von Tutschek took off in Dr I 404/17 at about 1015 hrs, leading Blumenbach, Hoffmann and several others. They were spotted by a patrol of five SE 5 pilots (from their old opponents, No 24 Sqn), and Lt H B Redler crossed to the east of what he described as a group of three triplanes and three Albatros Scouts going west, and then climbed into the sun. He then 'dived on the highest triplane and put 40 rounds down to colliding point. The EA stalled to the right and went down in a spin. The triplane was obviously out of control.'

The attack found von Tutschek and his pilots completely unprepared. Blumenbach and Hoffmann mistakenly thought they saw von Tutschek make a good landing, but he was found dead in the cockpit. When his body was removed, the cloth he normally used for wiping his goggles was

Striking tail and fuselage décor identified the triplane flown by Ltn Hans Müller of *Jagdstaffel* 15 in March 1918. Müller had used the black and white fuselage band on previous machines, and on his triplane this was extended to include the horizontal tail surfaces – as usual, the cowling was white. Note the additional gunsight affixed between the machine gun barrels. Müller accounted for two French two-seaters in January 1918 for his first claims, then went on to further glory with *Jasta* 18 (*USAF Museum*)

Four new triplanes of *Jasta* 15 are lined up at Autremencourt field in early March 1918. The first aircraft on the left bears a white fuselage band with black edging, while the next aircraft is Claus von Waldow's Dr I 412/17, marked with his 'N' emblem. At the extreme right is the Dr I of Ltn Hans Müller, identified by his black/white banded stripe and chevrons on the tailplane and elevators. All the aircraft bear white cowlings as unit insignia (*courtesy M Thiemeyer*)

still in place, knotted through a buttonhole and tucked under his safety harness, indicating that he had been completely surprised.

The death of von Tutschek hit the pilots and staff of JG II hard, particularly those of his cherished *Jasta* 12. The *Geschwader* had lost a popular and inspirational leader, but a more urgent issue existed – who would replace him? The *Kaiserschlacht* was only six days away, and there were few capable candidates. It had been decided that a *Jagdgeschwader Kommandeur* should be a regular army officer, preferably of hauptmann rank, and a veteran and skilled *Jagdflieger*. Fortunately, there was one such character of immense drive and determination waiting in the wings.

On the evening of the day after von Tutschek's death, a slim figure with his bandaged right arm in a sling arrived at Toulis – Hptm Rudolf Berthold had brought his stern and demanding guidance to JG II. The 26-year-old Berthold was already a legendary character in the ranks of German fighter aviation, commander of *Jasta* 18 with 27 victories and the *Pour le Mérite*. He had previously asked *Kogenluft* for a *Jagdgeschwader* command, but was still in recovery from his latest injuries suffered in October 1917. A festering wound rendered his right arm virtually useless, and he was forbidden to fly, but was a highly capable and aggressive CO. On 17 March JG II began the move to Guise under his leadership, which became official the next day. Great changes were in the making.

This unidentified Fokker of *Jasta* 15 forms a convenient backdrop for Ltn Hans Müller. The individual marking consists of two vertical white fuselage bands. In addition to the white cowling, the rudder is now painted a dark colour – apparently brown – as a *Jasta* marking, which would be applied to the unit's other triplanes. The open tray panel on the underside of the fuselage and the partially removed propeller cover indicate this machine was undergoing engine work. Next to the triplane is a Hannover CL type two-seater (*courtesy M Thiemeyer*)

OPERATION *MICHAEL*

With little time to waste, the fiercely determined Hptm Berthold quickly set to work instituting the move of JG II to the 18. *Armee,* commanded by *General der Infanterie* Oskar von Hutier. Before this was accomplished, though, Berthold managed to transfer some favourite comrades from his old *Jasta* 18 to *Jasta* 15, which would replace *Jasta* 12 as the *Stab Staffel* of JG II. Making the move were Oblt Ernst Wilhelm Turck (soon CO of *Jasta* 15), Ltn d R Josef Veltjens, and Ltn Oliver von Beaulieu-Marconnay. Ltn Walter Dingel was also brought in to serve as the new technical officer, and Vfw Hermann Margot became the communications officer. On 19 March all the *Geschwader* aircraft were flown to Guise. Berthold made the journey by car, as he was still grounded by a personal order from *Kogenluft.*

On 20 March, Berthold continued his efforts to retain the pilots of his former command. In order to transfer his trusted airmen of *Jasta* 18 to JG II, he simply switched the personnel of *Jasta* 15 en masse for those of *Jasta* 18. The 'Berthold Swap' was little more than a re-numbering process, which took place at Guise. The pilots of the 'old' *Jasta* 15 gave up their few Fokker triplanes and moved to Bruille in the 17. *Armee* sector, becoming the 'new' *Jasta* 18. These pilots included August Raben (the CO), Albert Mendel, Kurt Monnington, Hans Müller, Bergner, Glatz, Schleichardt, Spindler and von Waldow, and their association with JG II ends at this point.

Berthold and his men of *Jasta* 18 are seen about ten days before the switch with *Jasta* 15. Berthold is seated in the front, with his badly injured right arm in a sling. He had just returned to the unit, but was still unfit to fly, so he had brought his old friend Oblt Hans-Joachim Buddecke (to the right of Berthold, with one foot on the first step) over from *Jasta* 30 to lead the unit in the air. Buddecke arrived on 8 March, but was killed two days later, thus providing an approximate date for this photo. From left in the first row are Hermann Margot, Hugo Schäfer, Hans Burckhard von Buttlar, Josef Veltjens (with arm on Buttlar's shoulder), Berthold, Buddecke, Johannes Klein, and Arthur Rahn. In the back, from the left, are Georg von Hantelmann, Lohmann (OzbV), Ernst Wilhelm Turck, Walter Dingel (technical officer, arm in arm with Turck), Walther Kleffel (behind Buddecke), Theodor Weischer, and Oliver Freiherr von Beaulieu-Marconnay (with hand to hat)

Berthold's crowd forming the 'new' *Jasta* 15 included luminaries destined to play a major role in the epic of *Jagdgeschwader* II – Georg von Hantelmann, Arthur Rahn, Hugo Schäfer, Johannes Klein, Hans Burkhard von Buttlar, Theodor Weischer and Joachim von Ziegesar, along with the aforementioned Turck, Veltjens, von Beaulieu and Margot. These pilots would retain their Albatros and Pfalz machines painted in the unit markings (instituted by Berthold) of red noses and dark blue fuselages, as there was no time to convert to the rotary-engined Fokker Dr Is with the offensive scheduled for the very next day. Indeed, the urgency of the situation may help to explain how Berthold was able to pull off this stunt.

In any event, his close-knit band of pilots were now a vital part of the *Geschwader. Jagdstaffeln* 12, 13 and 19 were largely equipped with Fokker Dr Is by this time, although Albatros machines were still in use as well.

The *Jagdstaffeln* of the 18. *Armee* had been ordered to begin their participation in *Der Tag* at 0600 hrs. They were assigned to attack all hostile aircraft, enabling their own infantry contact and army co-operation machines to perform their tasks unhindered. JG II was specifically ordered to patrol at high altitude to achieve aerial domination on the left flank of the army, along with the 7. *Armee* fighter units to their south. From 0700 hrs, JG II pilots were also to undertake the destruction of enemy balloons, and were directed to rearm and refuel their aircraft as quickly as possible after their first sorties. Berthold was commanded to keep the *Kofl* of the 18. *Armee,* Hptm Alfred Streccius, constantly informed of the formation's readiness and strength throughout the day.

At 0450 hrs on 21 March 1918, some 6100 German guns opened fire on the batteries of the British Third and Fifth Armies behind the

Using his one good hand to hold his cigarette, Rudolf Berthold is given a light as he sits in the back seat of his staff car at *Jasta* 18 in early March. Directly to the right, behind the car, is Josef Veltjens, who was Berthold's protégé ever since they had served together in F. Fl. Abt. 23 in 1916. Just to the left of Berthold's head, framed by the doorway, is Georg von Hantelmann with the emblem of the Braunschweiger 'Death's Head' Hussars clearly visible on his dark cap. At this time Veltjens had ten victories, while von Hantelmann had yet to score, but they would both become great luminaries of JG II
(*Arthur Rahn collection, United States Air Force Museum*)

fog-bound trench lines, and Operation *Michael* was underway. After two hours, the gunfire was pulled back to hit the British infantry, and the trench mortars joined in the thunderous cascade – in five hours, 1.2 million shells were fired. German storm troopers left their trenches at 0940 hrs and rushed forward into the mist to begin their unprecedented advance. The same dense fog which aided the assault troops hampered aerial activities, and there was no flying until midday. In spite of great effort and enthusiasm, JG II scored no victories that day, nor indeed on the next.

23 March was a day of intense aerial combat along the whole 50-mile front, and Ulrich Neckel forced down the Sopwith Camel of 2Lt C H Clarke of No 70 Sqn. In the same fight Neckel's *Jasta* 12 comrade Vfw Dobberahn was wounded and left the *Staffel*. On the 25th Becker was credited with another Camel at St Christ. Two days later the 18. *Armee* took the French rail and road hub of Montdidier.

Jagdgeschwader II advanced along with the ground troops, and occupied the former Allied airfield at Balatre, near Roye, on the 28th. The group occupied the airfield complex with several other *Jagdstaffeln*. Joachim von Ziegesar of *Jasta* 15 wrote that:

'During his departure, "Tommy" had really attempted to set his hangars on fire, and yet the fire had gone out so that we found nearly intact homes for our beloved birds. Especially comfortable, though, were the lovely wooden barracks of the English officers. As usual, Hantelmann, Beaulieu and Schäfer – the "Three Inseparables" – bunked together in a hut, and I recall very clearly how on the first evening, roaring with delight, Beaulieu appeared in the mess with two half-destroyed gramophone records and Hantelmann showed up with a large tin of English marmalade, which they had flushed up from some corner or another. The happiness about the gramophone, at any rate, lasted longer than that for the marmalade!'

That same 28 March, two of Berthold's *Jasta* 15 protégés made their first marks in the *Geschwader* record books as Arthur Rahn downed a Bréguet (his 4th) and Hugo Schäfer brought down an RE 8 for his first of a string of 11 victories. The 23-year-old Schäfer (a former member of the 'Dancing Hussars' from Krefeld) had joined *Jasta* 18 in October. His

This *Jasta* 18 Albatros D V, photographed on a snowy field in early 1918, displays the personal marking of Arthur Rahn. It would continue to bear this insignia during its *Jasta* 15 career, even after Rahn left the unit for *Jasta* 19. The fuselage was the typical dark blue with a red nose, and blue may have also been applied to the uppersurfaces of the wings. Rahn's personal diamond band was applied in white against the dark blue background, but reversed to black on the pale blue underside. Rahn attained one of the first JG II victories for Berthold's transferees on 28 March, one week after the offensive began
(*Arthur Rahn collection, United States Air Force Museum*)

Offz-Stv Johannes Klein went to considerable trouble to personalise his *Jasta* 18/15 Albatros D V as evident here. It was fitted with a rear-view mirror and a rack for flare cartridges, and featured the usual unit markings of a red nose and dark blue fuselage. Joachim von Ziegesar's accounts indicate that Klein used a 'white belly band' as a personal marking, although on this machine it did not extend completely over the fuselage. Klein had already attained four victories in *Jasta* 18, and would go on to achieve 14 more in *Jasta* 15, and finish the war as an officer with the 'Hohenzollern'. He died in 1926 (*P M Grosz*)

aircraft were decorated with a white snake emblem. *Jasta* 13's Schmidt and Hildebrandt also gained victories on the 28th – a total of four for the *Geschwader*. Berthold had reason to be satisfied with all of his *Jagdstaffeln* except *Staffel* 19 (which had scored only once during its JG II career). On 29 March Rahn was transferred back into *Jasta* 19 (having served in the unit in 1917) to help build up its offensive potential.

The pace of aerial combat over the battlefront continued to intensify while the momentum of the ground advance began to stagnate. However, on 30 March the 18. *Armee* expanded its bridgehead across the Avre River and took Cantigny. Offz-Stv Johannes Klein (another of the Berthold crew from *Jasta* 18) sent a Bréguet down in flames over Montdidier on the 30th for his third victim. Less successful were Schneider of *Jasta* 13 and Pippart of *Jasta* 19, for both took hits in their engines and made forced landings.

31 March dawned with thunderstorms, but JG II nonetheless scrambled several times to intercept French aircraft. *Jasta* 19 made up for its former poor showing, as two SPADs were claimed by Vfw Gerdes and

Ltn d R Hans Körner had flown with Walter Göttsch in *Jasta* 8, and had attained his first victory with the unit on 10 January 1917. He then spent a brief interlude in Macedonia with Fl. Abt. (A) 246, where he achieved his second victory as a two-seater pilot, before eventually returning to *Jasta* 8. At Göttsch's request, he came to *Jasta* 19, where he flew this distinctive Dr I 503/17 marked with a white lightning bolt design on the fuselage sides and top. It was fitted with an Oigee telescopic sight affixed to two tubes bolted onto the machine gun mantels. Note that Körner had a central chin rest placed in between the guns in place of the normal MG butt padding. The wing cross appears to have been painted on a solid white panel, at least temporarily. Körner was a steady performer, and would add four more victories in *Jasta* 19 (*courtesy M Thiemeyer*)

The French Bréguet 14B2 bomber was a tough and dependable aircraft, and along with its reconnaissance version, the 14A2, would provide much of the opposition for JG II airmen in the spring and summer of 1918. This 14B2 (No 1346) was captured intact on 31 March 1918, apparently the victim of Ltn Walter Jumpelt of *Jasta* 19. The Gallic rooster on the fuselage identifies it as a machine from BR117, and the crew of Sgts Kerwood (American) and Biot were both taken prisoner

Shortly before the large airfield at Balatre was abandoned due to the shelling of 12/13 April 1918, this line-up of 13 red and dark blue Albatros and Pfalz fighters of *Jasta* 15 was photographed. In the foreground is the Pfalz D IIIa marked with the emblem of *Kommandeur* Berthold, but the amount of flying he did in this machine at JG II was minimal at best – he was still in recovery from his arm wound. Next in line is the Albatros D V of Oblt Dingel, the *Geschwader* technical officer, marked with his pale blue band. The D V of *Jasta* 15 commander Oblt Turck is fourth, identified by his white comet, then the Albatros D V of Ltn von Bealieu-Marconnay, marked with the '4D' branding iron insignia of his old dragoon regiment. Sixth is an unidentified machine with white chevrons, then the D V of Johannes Klein. Eighth in line is the Albatros of Veltjens, with his white Indian arrow, then the Pfalz D IIIa of von Buttlar. At the end of the line is a Halberstadt CL II 'hack' two-seater, painted in the unit's red and blue colours

Ltn Hans Körner (the latter's third), Göttsch shot down an AR 2 two-seater for his 18th success and Ltn Walter Jumpelt brought down a Bréguet 14B2 behind the lines at Guerbigny. Jumpelt's victim was probably a bomber from *Escadrille* BR117, crewed by machine gunner Sgt Biot and pilot Sous-Lt Charles Kerwood. The latter, who was wounded, was an American in the 'Lafayette Flying Corps'. Both men were made PoWs. In addition, four SPADs were claimed west of Montdidier, Klein and Schäfer of *Jasta* 15 each downing one, as did Becker and Neckel. Both of the latter pilots now had eight victories apiece. It was the most successful day to date for JG II.

On 1 April the *Geschwader* continued to ravage Allied formations. *Jasta* 19 was successful, with two more Bréguets falling to Göttsch and the reliable Arthur Rahn – the latter pilot made 'ace' with this claim. *Jagdstaffel* 13's Pippart engaged in his speciality of balloon busting again for his ninth *Luftsieg*. Schäfer and Klein of *Jasta* 15 were enjoying a run of luck as each scored their third victory in four days. Klein shot down and killed Cpl Henry Woodward of SPA94, who was another American in French service, while Schäfer was credited with a British SE 5 from the newly formed RAF. The elation over these four successes was tempered by the loss of Ltn d R Hoffmann of *Jasta* 12, who was wounded in the pelvis and died the following day in the hospital at Nesle.

2 and 3 April saw a relative lull in the ground fighting, and poor weather restricted aerial action on the latter date. On the 4th the 18. *Armee* made

its final push, but could achieve few gains, and on the evening of the next day Ludendorff ordered the attacks to stop. Operation *Michael* had ended, but the struggle for control of the air continued. 10 April started out well as Veltjens of *Jasta* 15 made his first mark in the JG II record book with an 'RE 8', which fell between the trenches near Rouvrel (possibly an Armstrong-Whitworth FK 8 of No 35 Sqn, which was forced to land).

Jasta 19's Dr Is went aloft in the afternoon to supply escort for a flight of bombers from a *Kagohl* assigned to hit Amiens. During this sortie the *Staffel* lost its capable and respected commander when Ltn d R Walter Göttsch took the opportunity to attack a British two-seater.

Flying Dr I 419/17, Göttsch led several triplanes down on the RE 8 of 2Lts H L Taylor (pilot) and W Lane of No 52 Sqn, which was flying at 500 metres. According to the British crew, the leading Fokker opened fire at about 100 yards, and Lane replied with his Lewis gun. In the ensuing exchange of shots, Lane was wounded in the head and Taylor in the leg, but they claimed the triplane spun away out of control and crashed. The RAF crew remained hard-pressed by the rest of *Jasta* 19, and they claimed they brought down another Dr I in flames (although only one triplane was destroyed) before they too were forced down. Taylor landed his RE 8 by the Bois de Gentelles, and near the burnt wreckage of the triplane.

The JG II account, however, states that after Göttsch had brought down the RE, he was flying low behind British lines when his Dr I was observed to slip or skid out of a right-hand bank and crash to earth, where it burst into flames. The *Jasta* pilots assumed that he had been hit by ground fire. The Germans gave Göttsch posthumous credit for the RE 8 to take his score to 20, while the RAF credited Lane and Taylor with bringing down the ace. Taylor saw the body, and said Göttsch was killed by a bullet before he hit the ground. The RAF pilot received treatment for his minor leg wound and soon returned to duty, and it was Taylor himself who dropped a message over the German lines ten days later, giving details of Göttsch's death.

The airfield at Balatre was home to about 150 German aircraft, which did not escape the notice of the enemy. At about noon on 11 April an Allied bombing squadron came over at high altitude and hit the village and the aerodrome. This event had been repeated several times, by day and night, since the *Geschwader* had occupied the field.

On 12 April Johannes Klein continued his recent victory skein by downing a SPAD two-seater at 1525 hrs near Ouvillers. The same day, the

A view of the other end of the same *Jasta* 15 line seen on page 28 reveals a Pfalz D IIIa marked with a white six-pointed star emblem at the extreme left (the Halberstadt CL II is just out of view). Next to the Pfalz is an Albatros D V still displaying Rahn's personal diamond marking, although Rahn had joined *Jasta* 19 by this time – both the Pfalz and this D V seem to have dark blue wings as well as fuselages. Next is an Albatros bearing a white lightning bolt emblem, and another with an unidentified oval insignia. The Pfalz D IIIa of von Buttlar is next in the line-up, featuring his hunting horn insignia. Then comes Veltjens' D V, Klein's machine, von Beaulieu's Albatros with its '4D' emblem and Turck's and Dingel's machines. Berthold's Pfalz D IIIa is seen at the end in front of the hangars. Note that all the aircraft are marked with *Balkenkreuz* insignia with broad white borders
(*Arthur Rahn collection, United States Air Force Museum*)

two aces Becker and Neckel maintained their parallel scores as *Jasta* 12 intercepted a formation of two-seaters, and their escorts, at about 4000 metres near the aerodrome. Becker got another 'SPAD two-seater' and Neckel was credited with a SPAD fighter (probably MdL Busch of SPA94, who was killed) at Villers-Brettoneux to bring their tallies to nine.

As early as 6 April, nine examples of the new Siemens-Schuckert Werke (SSW) D III (serial numbers 8346/17 to 8354/17) fighter began to join JG II. These unique, barrel-like scouts must certainly have evoked intense scrutiny from the *Geschwader* pilots. They were built around the radical 11-cylinder Siemens-Halske Sh III counter-rotary engine, which saw the propeller and cylinders rotate in an opposite direction to the crankshaft at 900 rpm. A four-bladed propeller with a large spinner was mounted on this engine, which together with the stocky sesquiplane design gave the D III an extremely pugnacious appearance.

By 18 May 26 more SSW D IIIs and one D IV had been delivered to the JG II pilots, who were initially enthralled with the new aeroplane's performance. One *Jasta* 15 flier reported, 'the D III is highly sensitive on the controls, possesses excellent flying qualities and climbs like a rocket!' On 22 April, Hptm Berthold told a visiting SSW engineer that the D III possessed a 'brilliant' rate of climb, and that the combination of the D III airframe and Sh III engine was 'faultless'. To keep the type's secrets safe, the JG II airmen were prohibited from flying it across the frontlines. Still, Berthold felt the D III had 'earned the trust of the pilots'. This trust would prove misplaced, however, as engine troubles soon began to surface.

BOMBARDMENT

The close proximity of Balatre aerodrome to the frontlines brought a rude awakening to the *Geschwader* on the night of 12/13 April 1918, when French artillery shelled the airfield with great effect. Hermann Becker gave this description of the events in a letter home:

'Because it had brightened up towards the end of the day, we had already reckoned we might be greeted by a nightly bombing. We had hardly gone to bed at 1030 hrs, when outside the flak fire began, and you could hear the noise of an aircraft. Some cautious men got up in order to go to the shelters (the trenches), but most of us – me included – stayed in

A heterogeneous set of insignia is seen on this group of *Jasta* 12 triplanes. The two on the left display the classic black tail and white cowling unit markings, with personal insignia of a black/white chevron and a white band. The Dr I in the foreground does not as yet bear any unit markings, but is also marked with a white band. Most curiously, the upper wing crosses are in the first form of *Balkenkreuz* insignia adopted by JG II, which has not yet been painted on the other triplanes in the photo – perhaps the upper wing was a replaced component from another machine. The order to replace the iron cross type insignia with straight-sided crosses was dated 17 March 1918, and was to be effected by 15 April

A resplendent group of ten Dr Is from *Jasta* 19 show off their unit and personal markings in this classic official photo, taken at Balatre around 10–12 April. First on the right is Arthur Rahn's 433/17, identified by his white diamond band and deputy leader's streamer affixed to the rudder. Third in line is Rienau's Dr I 504/17. At the far end are two SSW D IIIs. All these triplanes display the black/yellow banded tails and white cowlings of *Jagdstaffel* 19. On the fuselages, the national insignia was painted over with a streaky olive-brown camouflage closely approximating the factory finish, so the personal insignia would not conflict with the crosses

The mixed equipment of JG II during the *Kaiserschlacht* is evident in this view of Balatre airfield. Walter Göttsch's Fokker Dr I 419/17, with its white upper wing, is at left undergoing repair and maintenance. The cowling and machine guns have been removed, and the latter are seen beneath the starboard wings. At right is Siemens-Schuckert Werke D III 8346/17, supplied to *Jasta* 19 in April, which has just had its tail cross converted to *Balkenkreuz* format. This aircraft was also intended for use by Göttsch, and would soon have its fuselage painted white. Albatros fighters are seen in the distance (*HAC/UTD*)

bed, for most likely the fellow wouldn't drop his "eggs" exactly on our barracks. It did not take long until the first explosion. The thing could not have been far off, for the whole building shook and pieces of dirt clattered on the roof. One simply crawled a bit deeper under the covers and waited for the second "egg". But that one took a long time coming, although the machine was right over our heads.

'Perhaps five minutes had passed, then we heard another crash, this time a bit more to the side, but also between our sheds and the airfield. Strange, that whining sound, which had already struck us as odd the first time, for bombs usually announce their arrival with a rush, especially such big ones as these seemed to be according to the noise of their explosions. However, we trusted to our fate, until it dawned on us that the sound of the aircraft was no longer audible, and that the explosions followed each other faster and faster. Then someone rushed into our shed and yelled, "The field is being shelled with heavy artillery with aerial observation!"

'And now, out! We sprinted toward the still un-roofed trench, which was about 1¹/₂ metres deep – the roofed bomb shelters were already over-crowded with people. We preferred to stay in the trench, which was no protection against a direct hit, but at least provided cover against splinters. Shell after shell roared over us, bursting in front of us, and then behind us again. We strained hard in bending our knees very deeply.

There – *bang* – all of us were shaken and covered by earth. That seemed to be very, very close. Now the game grew unpleasant. Probably the next shell would land in our trench. There was nothing we could do but wait helplessly, though all of our bones ached because of the tight crouching in the wet trench.

'The bastards systematically worked over the entire airfield. The fire didn't lessen until 0500 hrs. We once left our trench, after midnight, because a shell had ignited a shed between our barracks in which 500 litres of fuel had been stored and also our two pigs and fifteen hens. There was nothing to be saved. The fuel was lost and only a few carbonised hunks of our hens remained. The pigs remained alive, although so badly burnt we had to slaughter them the next day.

'In spite of the continuous rain of shells, our main concern was to save the horses and cattle in the next shed, as well as equipment and luggage. This work went well, although we constantly had to lay down in the mud as soon as the shells roared over. When we had finished the salvage of everything, and were again crouching in our trench, a shell exploded right in the hangar of another *Staffel*, which was immediately set ablaze. Exploding ammunition and signal-lights produced a crackling bonfire. There was no chance of saving the machines, which had been filled with fuel. Six valuable Albatros were burnt there.'

In the light of morning, the dazed *Geschwader* personnel took a sobering look at the damage, and sadly realised it was far greater than they had imagined. The aerodrome had been hit by about 200 shells, and *Jagdgeschwader* II had 25 aeroplanes destroyed or damaged but incredibly not one human fatality. The *Geschwader* was largely out of action for the next three weeks, claiming only two victories during the rest of the month. An airfield relocation was of obvious necessity, and the group moved to Bonneuil Ferme on the 13th, then to Les Mesnil, near Nesle, on the 21st, remaining with the 18. *Armee*.

This hangar was one of those damaged on the night of 12/13 April 1918 when the JG II airfield at Balatre, near Roye, was heavily shelled by French artillery. About 200 shells fell on the field and the *Geschwader* lost 25 aeroplanes damaged or destroyed. Two Albatros D Vs, probably from *Jasta* 12, are visible in the dark area at left

Groundcrews move a Fokker Dr I of *Jasta* 12 past a hangar at Balatre. The triplane displays the April 1918 version of the *Balkenkreuz* insignia applied to the black rear fuselage and the formerly black rudder, now overpainted white in response to the *Kogenluft* directive of 17 March

After the death of Göttsch, Arthur Rahn served as acting CO of *Jagdstaffel* 19 for a few days. On 18 April Hans Pippart was transferred from *Jasta* 13 to lead *Jasta* 19. Pippart's new responsibilities must have agreed with him, for he sealed the takeover of his new *Staffel* by achieving his tenth victory on 20 April. This began a four-month scoring surge that would take his tally to 22.

The next day a formation of Bréguets from *Escadrille* BR220 crossed the lines in the Noyon–Montdidier region and pressed through to St Quentin. *Jasta* 12 waylaid the formation, and the recently-promoted Ltn d R Ulrich Neckel brought one down (probably flown by MdL de Conflans and Asp Millardet) to become a ten-victory *Kanone*. The day's success was marred by an unsettling message received in the afternoon. In the 2. *Armee* sector to the north, Manfred von Richthofen had failed to return from a patrol.

The grimly determined Berthold wrote, 'Richthofen's killed, daily the comrades fall, the English are (numerically) superior. I must show the young

SSW D III 8346/17 was one of nine issued to JG II on 6 April 1918, and is seen here at Balatre with *Jasta* 19 triplanes in the distance. The scout had its fuselage, tailplane and fin painted white for its intended use by *Staffelführer* Walter Göttsch, but he probably never flew the machine in combat prior to his death on 10 April. This photo and others were reportedly taken ten days later. The crosses on wings and rudder have been converted to an early style of *Balkenkreuz*, and the five-colour lozenge fabric on the wings and elevator is clearly evident (*P M Grosz*)

RUDOLF BERTHOLD

The son of a Franconian forester, Rudolf Berthold was born on 24 March 1881 at Ditterswind, near Bamberg. He entered the army pre-war, and was commissioned in the *Infanterie-Regiment* Nr 20, *'Graf Tauentzien'*. He started the war as an observer in F. Fl. Abt. 23, with whom his reconnaissance reports during the Battle of the Marne earned him recognition. By November 1914 Berthold had started pilot training, and he soon returned to his unit and began flying twin-engined AEGs in combat. After several bad experiences with the AEGs, he happily switched to a Fokker Eindecker.

Berthold became a member of the fighter detachment formed from F. Fl. Abt. 23, designated *Kampfeinsitzer-Kommando-Vaux,* and on 2 February 1916 he attained his first victory. By 16 April his tally stood at five, but on the 25th he crashed in a Pfalz E IV, sustaining a severe skull injury and a broken nose, thigh and pelvis, as well as a concussion. With typical stubborn determination he was back in the air by August, scoring a sixth time on the 24th which led to the 'Hohenzollern'. Berthold continued his successes after *KEK Vaux* was transformed into *Jasta* 4, and received the *Pour le Mérite* on 10 October.

His fierce drive and sterling record were rewarded with command of *Jasta* 14 six days later. Here, he honed his aggressive leadership skills and downed three opponents in April, but was lightly wounded again on the 24th. A more serious wound on 23 May put him out of action until August, when he took over *Jasta* 18. There, he built a core of effective *Jagdflieger* who would follow him loyally, and he had his best month ever in September 1917 with 14 victories, bringing his total to 27. On 10 October 1917 Berthold sustained his third serious wound when his upper right arm bone was shattered. When he returned to *Jasta* 18 on 1 March 1918, he was in constant pain and unable to fly. However, he was still chosen to replace von Tutschek as head of JG II in March.

By the sheer force of his indomitable will, Berthold returned to flying, adding 16 more opponents to his record before crashing for a final time on 10 August. His flying was over, but not his fighting. During the tumultuous period following the armistice, this ardent nationalist formed and led a right-wing paramilitary *Freikorps* unit known as the *Eiserne Schar Berthold.* This 'Iron Host' earned a formidable reputation in the *Freikorps'* freebooting campaign in the Baltic States in 1919. In March 1920 Berthold led it south from Hamburg toward Berlin to take part in the Kapp-Lüttwitz *Putsch* – a doomed coup against the Weimar Republic. When the unit reached Harburg it was halted, and on 15 March it was surrounded by Reichswehr troops and armed civilian left-wing 'militia'. A newspaper report states that Berthold was taken prisoner, badly ill treated and shot. The story that he was strangled with the ribbon of his 'Blue Max' is no doubt propaganda, but he had indeed been murdered by his countrymen.

ones that duty stands above everything else.' One of those comrades who fell was Uffz Emil Dassenies from *Jasta* 13, who was observed to spin down after encountering an Allied aircraft on 23 April and was later reported dead.

For the rest of April aerial operations were hampered by the lack of aeroplanes and poor weather, although the unit still provided escort for two-seaters doing photographic and reconnaissance work.

Left
Rudolf Berthold earned fame as a Fokker Eindecker pilot and received his *Pour le Mérite* in October 1916. That award is evidenced in this Sanke card portrait, which depicts him as a relatively healthy oberleutnant. He was one of the few such early aces to survive into 1918, rising to the rank of hauptmann and command of JG II
(*courtesy L Bronnenkant*)

This view of Balatre airfield in early April shows Oblt Blumenbach's Dr I 217/17 at left, after the insignia was changed to early *Balkenkreuz* style and the rudder re-painted white. The vertical white band that intersected the horizontal band is clearly in evidence. The other *Jasta* 12 triplane at right unusually has an iron cross insignia on a white field, and this may be a replacement component. A broad white fuselage band was applied in front of the black tail as a personal marking. The thin style of cross on a black field is evident on the wings and fuselage. In the background is a Siemens D III
(*photo and information courtesy A Imrie*)

PERSONNEL SHAKE-UP

The enforced inactivity gave Berthold the opportunity to do some unpleasant, but necessary, housekeeping. His festering right arm wound caused him constant intense pain, and splinters of bone continually worked out of the wound to the skin surface. He had not yet been able to return to flying, but he still commanded his group with an iron hand. The uncompromising *Geschwader* commander's leadership style had apparently caused dissension in the ranks and arguments with some of his *Jasta* leaders. On 25 April, Berthold wrote in a private letter to his sister:

'I have so many worries and annoyances. I must have three *Staffelführer* removed. It is a hard blow. Richthofen is dead as well – I am now the very last one. And instead of teamwork, one finds difficulties. It is ugly and wears you down. The *Staffelführer* had organised a type of plot in order to overthrow me – I will be ruthlessly hard. In the future I *will* fly again. The boys should be ashamed of themselves, and I can get the "sad brothers" out easier. The death of Richthofen has also dampened things. Now I have to get on with it like a member of the Old Guard. Maybe I'll get it, too.'

More details of this 'plot' are lacking, but three *Jasta* commanders were indeed replaced in the following weeks. On 1 May, Oblt Alex Thomas of *Jasta* 13 was sent off to command *Jasta* 69 in exchange for that unit's commander, Ltn d R Wilhelm Schwartz. As was customary, Thomas took three pilots along with him to his new unit – these were Hermann Schmidt, Otto Sarnighausen and Julius Weber. Schwartz brought Uffz Johannes Fritzsche with him from *Staffel* 69.

On 18 May, *Jasta* 12 leader Oblt Paul Blumenbach was transferred to command of *Jasta* 31. By order of *Kogenluft,* he was replaced by Ltn Robert Hildebrandt from *Jasta* 13. On the same day even Oblt Ernst Wilhelm Turck (one of Berthold's men from the old *Jasta* 18) was replaced as *Staffelführer* of *Jasta* 15 by Ltn d R Josef Veltjens. Although a career officer, Turck had gained only a single victory back in September

1917, while Berthold's favourite Veltjens had 13 by this time. Turck was transferred to command Saxon *Jasta* 54.

Berthold also found time to write up some answers to questions posed by *Kofl* of the 18. *Armee*. His memorandum of 28 April read;

'The task of the *Jagdgeschwader* is, in the first place, the energetic fighting of the enemy infantry co-operation and artillery (spotting) aircraft, and in the second place the attacking of enemy bombing formations. The *Geschwader* only takes its orders from the *Kofl*, who must be best informed on the hot spots in the sector by General Headquarters. Directives are made only by telephone. In addition, the *Geschwader* must have several *Luftschutz-Offiziere* (air defence officers) on strength, who are sent forward by the *Geschwader*. They are equipped with WT (wireless telephones). They immediately follow the infantry and are attached to a Flak unit.

'With their WT, they are to constantly inform the *Geschwader* about our own and the enemy's aerial activity. Demands requiring an increase in fights and victories must be made on the *Geschwader*. Therefore, the unit must be equipped with the best current machines and with young, dashing pilots who are not yet "used up".

'Difference between a *Geschwader* and a *Jagdgruppe* – the *Jagdgruppe* works closely with their own frontline (reconnaissance) machines. This demands their constant attention. Their working space is relatively small in order to be able to fulfil this demand, and must be in the area of the attacking force. The *Jagdgeschwader* works for the entire army, prevents the work of enemy infantry and artillery aircraft and protects the work of the *Jagdgruppe* and two-seater units indirectly by constant attacks on single-seater formations and by victories. The *Jagdgruppe* flies when the two-seaters are working. The *Geschwader* flies mainly when the enemy is up in strength.

'More than any other flying unit, the *Jagdgeschwader* must be mobile. It must be in a position to stay close with the infantry if it wants to energetically attack low-flying infantry and artillery machines. The types of cars and lorries which are now available are completely unsuitable for those demands, especially because there are constant breakdowns due to bad material. It would be advisable for a lorry column to be attached.'

Under Berthold's resolute command, JG II would account for 19 French aircraft and balloons in May. On the 2nd, *Jasta* 19 commander

Oblt Ernst Wilhelm Turck was commander of *Jasta* 18 at the time Berthold took over JG II, and thus he became the leader of *Jasta* 15 after 20 March 1918. He is seen here in his splendid *Jasta* 18 Albatros D V, bearing the 'Berthold colours' of a red nose and dark blue fuselage, with a light blue underside. The stylish white comet emblem was Turck's personal insignia, and the wings were finished in green and mauve camouflage. Like other *Jasta* 18 Albatros and Pfalz fighters, this aircraft was transferred to *Jasta* 15 along with its pilot, and was photographed on Balatre airfield with the early style of *Balkenkreuz* insignia. Turck scored only one victory, and was transferred out of *Jasta* 15 in May by the results-oriented Berthold (*A Imrie via HAC/UTD*)

Ltn d R Rudolf Rienau was a longtime *Jasta* 19 pilot, having joined the unit at the end of October 1917. His Fokker Dr I 504/17 was identified by striking white diagonal stripes, and the *Staffel* markings are evident on the tailplane and elevator. Rienau would survive a parachute jump on 13 September 1918, and finish the war with a score of six. He became a flight instructor in the early 1920s, but was killed in a flying accident in Berlin on 23 May 1925 (*courtesy M Thiemeyer*)

A study in concentrated energy. Ltn d L Hans Pippart is helped into his *Fliegerkombination* as he prepares for a flight in his Dr I 471/17. Pippart took command of *Jasta* 19 on 18 April following the death of Göttsch. Thus began the most successful period of his career, when he would score 13 times in four months. The triplane appears to be painted a solid dark colour (black?) on the uppersurfaces of the fuselage and all wings, but still displays the white cowling of *Jasta* 19. A personal emblem of a disc, perhaps in yellow, is seen on the fuselage side and top decking, and this was repeated on the centre section of the top wing. Auxiliary central sights are mounted between the guns, and a Morell anemometer airspeed indicator is fitted to the starboard interplane strut (*courtesy M Thiemeyer*)

Hans Pippart had double reason for celebration. He earned the prestigious 'Hohenzollern', and at 1315 hrs he destroyed a Bréguet 14B2 from BR126 for his 11th victory.

At 2000 hrs on 4 May Pippart scored again as he led a patrol of *Jasta* 19 triplanes down onto three SPADs from SPA77 that had been attacking a German balloon behind the Montdidier salient. Pippart singled out the SPAD of American Cpl Thomas Buffum, who many years later gave this account:

'I looked up and the ceiling of clouds just above appeared to be raining black Fokker triplanes. Instinctively, I pulled my SPAD into a tight climbing spiral and opened up on the first one that came into my machine guns' sights. While making an Immelmann turn to shake off a very persistent fellow on my tail, I heard a crash followed by a loud roaring. I realised that I was on fire. A great feeling of rage filled me. The pressure gauge for the gas tank read zero. I switched on the gravity feed emergency tank in the top wing, and as the spluttering motor picked up again, I threw the aeroplane into a side slip. This kept the flames away from the cockpit. Another bullet exploded the emergency gas tank practically in my face.

'It looked as if everything was all up as I ducked down into the cockpit and a sheet of flames swept over my head. My aeroplane was less than 100 ft above a large grove of trees, but – oh, what luck – on my right was a nice open field. With the first thud of the wheels on the ground, I was out of the cockpit and landed on my feet. The machine rolled on for a distance and, already a mass of flames, came to rest between shell holes. My helmet and forehead were singed, but otherwise I appeared to be unhurt.'

Buffum looked up in time to see the SPAD of his comrade Cpl Laraud burst into flames under the fire of Arthur Rahn (his sixth victory) and

crash in the next field. One of the triplane pilots flew low overhead and waved to Buffum as he was taken prisoner by German artillerymen.

4 May also brought more staff changes. Ltn Eitel-Friedrich Rödiger *Freiherr* von Manteuffel became the new adjutant, as Oblt Heinz Krapfenbauer had been given the job of *Nachrichten Offizier* (intelligence officer). Ltn Dingel's technical department now came under the control of the adjutant, with Vfw Margot as assistant.

Two days later *Jasta* 13 had a field day, with commander Wilhelm Schwartz and Ltn Robert Hildebrandt both flaming Bréguets from *Escadrille* BR131 at around 1720 hrs. Three hours later Hans Pippart continued his own string of destruction with a SPAD – probably the machine of the commander of SPA96, Lt Maurice Barthe, who was killed. Hermann Becker of *Jasta* 12 also downed a notable Frenchman that day. He shot down a SPAD VII probably flown by Lt Jean Chaput, the 16-victory commander of SPA57. As was the custom, Becker casually called his French opponent a 'Tommy' when he wrote:

'My triplane was attacked by a Tommy, whereupon my guns jammed (temporarily). Despite this, I attacked him again and again. I repeated this until he went down over a forest, landing on a path between the trees.'

Although he had managed to land his SPAD, Chaput bled to death from a wound in his femoral artery. Four victories on this 6th of May were balanced by the loss of Flg Görzel of *Jasta* 19, who was made a PoW.

Berthold's command skills resulted in his being entrusted with the entire operational deployment of all fighters in the 18. *Armee* on 8 May, under the direction of *Kofl.* The succeeding day, Becker shot down his third Frenchman in a week south-west of Faverolles. On 10 May, Veltjens continued his own 'hot streak' by downing the SPAD of Adj Henri Chan of SPA 94 to bring his tally to 12. The frenetic pace of combat persisted, as the new commander of *Jasta* 13, Ltn d R Wilhelm Schwartz, scored his fourth victory on the 15th with a Bréguet sent down to a flaming crash at Quesmy, near Guiscard.

Following his transfer back to his old *Jasta* 19 from *Jasta* 15 in late March, Arthur Rahn continued to use his white diamond band personal insignia on Dr I 433/17, as seen here. Interestingly, the port wheel cover appears to be white, along with the engine cowling – an aspect not evident in other views of this triplane. Rahn's personal marking of diamonds flanked by white bands seems to have been painted directly onto the camouflaged fuselage. Following his wounding on 17 July 1918, Rahn did not return to combat, but was awarded the 'Hohenzollern' on 1 August. It was a bit unusual at this late date for a pilot with 'only' six victories to receive the Order, but Rahn's lengthy and steady service undoubtedly entered into the equation (*Arthur Rahn collection, United States Air Force Museum*)

On 18 May another Bréguet fell to Veltjens, who took command of *Jasta* 15 that same day. Fortunately, his trusted pilot Joachim von Ziegesar left several evocative accounts of the close-knit band of hunters which made up the *Staffel*, namely the tall 'Seppl' Veltjens, talkative von Beaulieu-Marconnay (known as 'Bauli' or 'Beauli'), the ever-somnolent Johannes Klein, playful and boyish Georg von Hantelmann and others. Von Ziegesar recounted the events of 18 May in Walter Zuerl's *Pour le Mérite Flieger* (translated by O'Brien Browne):

"'Say, Klein. You're sorry that the day doesn't have 26 hours so that you could sleep a bit more, right?'

"'Oh nonsense. You call this flying? What good is this pretty aeroplane to me when I can't even go up to the front in it? One day the Frenchies will get my aircraft for sure – what nonsense!'

"'Calm down now. A fellow can't sleep at all!'"

Josef 'Seppl' Veltjens took command of *Jagdstaffel* 15 after Oblt Turck was transferred to *Jasta* 54 to serve as its CO on 18 May 1918. Long a comrade of Berthold's, Veltjens is seen in his Albatros D V while still at *Jasta* 18. He continued to fly this machine, decorated with his familiar 'Indian arrow', after transferring to *Jasta* 15 in March. Veltjens added four victims to his tally in April and May, but his scoring rate would really blossom once he obtained a Fokker D VII

After taking command of JG II Berthold began to put his own indelible stamp on the appearance of the *Geschwader* by instituting new unit markings throughout the formation, although these would take some time to be fully implemented. Like Berthold's *Jasta* 15, every *Staffel* in JG II would eventually be flying aircraft with blue fuselages and tailplanes, but each was identified by its own cowling colour – *Jasta* 15 retained its traditional red cowlings, *Jasta* 12 had white, *Jasta* 13 had dark green and *Jasta* 19 used yellow. An early example of the *Jasta* 13 marking is apparently seen on this Fokker Dr I 193/17, flown by the *Staffelführer* Ltn d R Wilhelm Schwartz. The triplane was photographed just after Schwartz had shot down a Bréguet over Quesmy, near Guiscard, on 15 May 1918. It certainly looks to bear a blue fuselage and dark green cowling, but oddly enough the cross format seen is quite out of date by this time *(HAC/UTD)*

This rare shot of JG II 'in action' shows Albatros fighters of *Jasta* 15 just at the point of taking off. At right is the D V flown by Oliver von Beaulieu-Marconnay, his white branding iron insignia very evident. To its left is another D V, bearing the white chevron-style marking of an unknown pilot. Both of these machines display dark green and mauve painted camouflage patterns on their wings and the *Staffel* markings of dark blue fuselage and tails with red noses (*Arthur Rahn collection, United States Air Force Museum*)

'Despite this sullen admonition from someone with a sleepy disposition, the seven pilots of *Jagdstaffel* 15 could certainly not hold their tongues. Instead, the conversation flowed out energetically. Indeed, there was a topic to talk about – the new aeroplanes, SSW D IIIs! The things were parked over there, in front of the grey tents. They looked absolutely swanky and strong. The huge rotary engine with its 11 bulky cylinders totally displaced the almost delicate-seeming construction of this generally stable aircraft, with its fat and sturdy fuselage, as if it had been stuffed full. Anything other than the mighty four-bladed propeller would have appeared ridiculous on this bulky steel monster.

'The conversations of the *Jasta* 15 pilots, who are lying down or sitting against the wall of a tent, concerned this aircraft which had arrived at the beginning of May 1918 to be tried out by the *Staffel*. They had already had to give up their good old Albatros machines, in part, and it was forbidden to fly to the front with the new aeroplanes. So there was nothing left but to wait, in a bad mood, next to the crates, all ready to take off, until an enemy squadron dared to enter the German hinterland.

'It is May and the French sun favours them in the early afternoon. The conversation slowly dies down. Naturally, "Bauli" cannot, as usual, keep his mouth shut. Now he has to tickle his best friend Hugo Schäfer's nose with a stalk of grass as he stretches out on his back, sleeping softly.

'Ha! – far, far away at the front tiny clouds from explosions appear at a great height. A blow from "Bauli's" small, hard fist on Seppl's unendingly long limbs wakes him up with a start. "Hey, Seppl. Flak – look there!" In a second, everybody is on their feet.

'"Where? I don't see anything."

'"*There*, boy – four, five, eight, ten. Damn! How many are they, then? Kids, they're coming this way!"

'"Let's go!" yells Seppl, who is leading the *Staffel*. Hustle and bustle. The good mechanics have already appeared on the scene because of the approaching flak fire. Into the fur coats! Barely a second later everybody is sitting in their aircraft. While the mechanics fasten the seat belts, a couple of strokes on the oil pump, petrol switch on, fuel lever okay. "On!" The strongest and most experienced of the mechanics grasp the propeller blades. The engine doesn't start. Doesn't want to.

'A quick glance at the increasing clouds of shrapnel which indicate the position of the enemy squadron that is apparently approaching at an extreme height, and once again: "On!" Prr, prr. Ha! Shaking, vibrating, blue fumes of stinking castor oil (thanks to the fleeing Tommies!), rattling, pulling power, unbelievably tamed. Quickly – let the ignition button out a bit longer – 890 revs! Good. "Take 'em away!" Away fly the chocks in front of the wheels and 160 hp pushes forward its fragile structure of dry wood and linen.

'In a second the ground disappears beneath the wheels. All right. Now the pilot is once again one with his craft. The roaring of the engine seems delightful to his ears. There they are, up above. Now, show what you can do, little aeroplane – I want to be up there, having at the cockades. The will of the pilot lives in his aircraft. In seconds, a heavy load of tons is lifted hundreds of metres high. It is as if you're giddy. You can watch the movements of the needle on the altitude meter. But wait – what's happened to the good old *Staffel* discipline? Where are my comrades? Ah, here comes the "snake" – Hugo Schäfer – and there, too, is Klein with his white belly band. Now, then, at them – but be sure not to lose any height.

'Two minutes after take-off – 2000 metres. The three move together. Now you can already see the enemy squadron better. It's making right for our own airfield – 24 enemy bombers. Now just wait, you fellows – we're also here, and even more quickly than we had imagined. If we could catch you before you reach our airfield – but you're much too high. But the SSW climbs! She hangs on her propeller. Over there one of the broad, bright red noses is stretching up into the heights. Oh, and over there is Seppl already – a pity that he's so far away.

'Seven minutes after take off – altimeter at 3800! And the brothers are still above us. We're tight after them. A glance at the earth. Damn, mushroom clouds are already growing out of the ground near our

This aircraft was one of the early SSW D IIIs supplied to *Jasta* 15, being flown by Joachim von Ziegesar in May 1918. Its fuselage was painted dark blue, but the wide-bordered *Balkenkreuz* remains fairly discernible. The cowling was red. The pilot's personal emblem consisted of three white feathers. The wing crosses were now extended to full chord length, and the wings and elevator retained their five-colour printed fabric finish. Von Ziegesar was probably flying this machine on 18 May when he saw Veltjens score his 13th victory

airfield. Rage!! We are still 200 metres too low. And the 96 eyes up there have seen us, too. Back and forth movements begin in the tightly flying group – a bit nervous, or what? They are turning! Another pull on the fuel lever, push a bit, and it's up with the crate. One-hundred metres higher, the tightly formed enemy wedge is coming on. Turn around and come in from behind? No. Pull up, in the crosshairs a teeming flock – now one's in the crosshairs and the machine guns rattle in exultation.

'The desire to see the opponent crash is too powerful. The still unfamiliar aircraft is pushed too far and spins – damn, what's going on? In a rapid turn, the aircraft rushes down. A situation never experienced before. The wings bend and the wires beat with a whine. Petrol off, centre the stick! This witches' dance continues! Petrol on for a bit, dive! The speed is increasing. Again petrol, stick forward, confusion. Wait a second – here she comes – the controls are responding again, the engine is pulling. Well, what an odd thing. Everything is okay. Where are the others? Up there. Yes, this incomprehensible bit of fun cost 1000 metres of height.

'But now once again to it. After them, pull up and dive. Disarray has come to the enemy formation – thus it seems as if my comrades have indeed done something to them during my ride on the carousel. I can still make out four red and blue Siemens (the colours of Berthold's *Staffel*). At the same height, I am about 200 metres from the enemy again. A pity my crate is not faster! Now three craft are moving out of the grouping. Now, dive so that the engine cries. It doesn't matter if there is a red warning line on the tachometer. Now I'm there.

'Pull up under the last one! So strong are the vibrations of my aircraft that it is not possible to aim correctly. I am sitting tightly behind him, undercarriage in the sights, a bit higher, let off a burst. Only a couple of bursts and the familiar petrol trail comes spraying out of the opponent's stricken tank. Excitedly, and keeping him in sight, I turn around in order to force him down on to our territory when suddenly – "pop, pop, bang, crack!" Good God! Petrol in my face, goggles hit and still the observer's machine gun bullets whistle around me on the right as I hurry downwards at a thundering speed to the homeland. Veltjens bags the Bréguet I had fired at as his 13th, and I came home with many hits, a shot up fuel tank, and tattered glory as the first one of us to have done a flat spin.'

On that same 18 May, Hildebrandt took over command of *Jasta* 12 by order of *Kogenluft*. Although he had received his 'Hohenzollern' that very day, Hermann Becker was disappointed that he had not been appointed *Staffelführer*, and he complained bitterly:

'I thought this was very unfair, since Hildebrandt only had three victories. So Berthold, who felt I should have had *Jasta* 12 with my 11 victories, sent me home on leave until he could argue this injustice with *Kofl*. In the meantime, this robbed me of valuable weeks where a lot of victories could be gained.'

Becker's lucky streak was indeed broken, and he would not score again until August.

There was probably a bit of a celebration on 20 May, as news arrived that Veltjens had also received the 'Hohenzollern' – the third award of the Order to a JG II pilot in less than three weeks. With 57 confirmed victories, the young pilots could be proud of their contribution to Ludendorff's offensive.

EQUIPMENT TROUBLES

Jagdgeschwader II had taken no active part in Ludendorff's second offensive (Operation *Georgette*) to the north, but in late May the group began preparations for its role in the third offensive of 1918 (Operation *Blücher*). This would primarily involve the German 7. *Armee* immediately on the left of the 18. *Armee*, as well as the 1. *Armee* further south. It would be known as the Chemin des Dames Offensive, or the Aisne Offensive. As Berthold readied his *Geschwader* for the assault, he may have reflected that with four loyal *Jasta* leaders in place, his group was well in hand. He was also fiercely determined to return to the air himself.

All was not well with the group's aircraft, however. Although initially promising, the performance of the SSW D III machines was deteriorating. Their engines showed troubling signs of failure after seven to ten hours of use, the synthetic castor oil substitute *Voltol* contributing to over-heating and eventual engine seizure. The Sh III engine had evidently been prematurely rushed into service, and was not yet ready for the demands of combat use. The disillusioned pilots of JG II even composed an amusing bit of doggerel about the engine problems, based on 'The Ten Little Indians' (translated by Rick Duiven):

'Ten little Siemens were circling around a barn,
A piston ring froze up tight, nine were left without harm.
Nine little Siemens were playing out to join the hunt,
The spark plugs flew away from one, eight are left to hunt.
Eight little Siemens, they flew up very high,
A piston went out fast, now only seven are all right.
Seven little Siemens were flying on top of a spot,
The magneto didn't turn on one, only six are left on lot.
From six little Siemens flew out one with red socks,
Connecting rod salad right away, only five came back to box.
Five little Siemens we still have left to fly,
A throttle valve failed, but four still take the sky.
Four little Siemens were flying high and free,
A cylinder turned blue, we now only have three.
Three little Siemens are going very fast,
The bearings blow out quickly, only two who pass the test.
Two little Siemens, flying lonely like father and son,
An engine seizes completely tight, and now there's only one.
One little Siemens went up in brave salute,
He came up only 3000 metres and now too is *kaputt*!'

The moral of the poem was, 'For us an engine that devours itself so quickly is useless.'

Most of the flawed Siemens fighters were returned to the factory for modification in late May. Berthold submitted an objective evaluation of the type in the hope that, 'the Siemens fighter may be made available again for frontline use as quickly as possible for, after elimination of the present

Siemens-Schuckert Werke D III 8345/17, minus its rudder and spinner, sits forlornly on the Balatre airfield of JG II in April 1918. The hangar in the background appears to show damage from the shelling of the night of 12/13 April. Although the performance of the Siemens fighters seemed impressive at first, their engines revealed disturbing failures after only seven to ten hours of use. The powerplants suffered from over-heating and piston seizure – some piston heads disintegrated and fell into the crankcases. Most of the SSW aircraft were sent back to the factory for engine replacement and airframe modification in May

faults, it is likely to become one of our most useful fighter aircraft'. The loss of these fighters left JG II in a bad way, as *Jagdstaffeln* 12 and 19 were temporarily rendered impotent. On 26 May the group's war diary reported, 'Two *Staffeln* without any aeroplanes'. The worn Fokker triplanes of the *Staffeln* were apparently retained or returned for use, but these machines had their own problems.

THE AISNE OFFENSIVE

Such difficulties mattered little in the 'big picture', however, and on 27 May the Chemin des Dames push was launched with great success. At 0100 hrs nearly 4000 German guns poured gas and explosive shells on to the French Sixth Army (which included five exhausted British divisions from the Somme) as well as the US 2nd Division. At 0400 hrs the German infantry of the 7. *Armee* moved up behind the barrage and took the centre of the Chemin des Dames in an hour. By evening they had crossed the Aisne and reached the Vesle. One day after the offensive started the storm troops had advanced 20 miles.

JG II was deployed to prevent enemy aircraft from penetrating into the areas of the 18. *Armee* and cover the right flank of the 7. *Armee*. The pilots were directed to fly in the upper air space for most of their patrols, only descending at the very end of their time aloft to attack the Allied infantry co-operation machines and artillery spotters. At this time the famous 'Paris Gun' was located on the left wing of the 18. *Armee,* and JG II also flew patrols to protect it from aerial detection.

By the second day of the offensive Berthold could hold himself back no longer. He had managed to acquire a brand new Fokker D VII from JG I, and said of the aircraft, 'Flies very comfortably. Above all, the controls are so light that I can even handle them with my right arm.' In spite of the festering wounds in his right arm and crippled hand, Berthold was helped into the D VII and took off to lead *Jasta* 15 into battle. In a letter to his sister, he reported:

'I have just now returned from a flight. Shot up a Frenchman. After a few shots, the opponent was finished. Altogether there were two. The man flying next to me shot down the second one. There is once again a ray of hope. Above all, because of this, I have a better grip on my *Geschwader*, and I can be more truthful to the little people (*Leutchen*) at *Kogenluft*. I believe it is going to be difficult for me to be successful in getting my *Geschwader* into the shape that I would like it to have, but I have resolved not to become angry. The pain was especially hard over the last two days.'

Berthold was credited with a Bréguet at Crouy, near Soissons, for his 29th victory, while his jubilant wingman Ltn von Beaulieu-Marconnay achieved confirmation for his very first triumph. On the same day, Flg Wilhelm Dombrowe of *Jasta* 12 crashed one of his unit's worn-out triplanes on the field at Mesnil and died of his injuries several hours later.

The *Geschwader* made 25 front flights on 29 May in spite of the dense haze and low clouds. Berthold led a *Jasta* 15 sortie into the darkening skies south of Soissons, and at about 1830 hrs they were surprised by a French SPAD formation which dived on them. In the ensuing fight Berthold, Veltjens and von Hantelmann each sent down a SPAD (Hantelmann's was only credited as 'forced to land'), and soon after Berthold despatched a Salmson 2A2. The German ace was almost lost, however, as he wrote:

'I shot down my 30th and 31st within ten minutes – one of them over his own airfield. I would have almost stayed over there in this show, as I had shot my own propeller. Oh well, everything turned out well this time. Sadly, during all this, the motor also went bust, so that I am at the moment without an aircraft. One sees that I haven't quite forgotten air fighting. I think, though, that for a long time yet I am still going to have a lot of trouble with my arm.'

As the temperatures increased, so did aircraft serviceability issues. Initially, there were only enough Fokker D VIIs to equip *Jasta* 15, and in the summer heat the Oberursel engines of the triplanes became increasingly unreliable. At times the lack of replacement triplanes took

Hptm Berthold managed to acquire the first Fokker D VII of JG II for himself in late May, and this early Fokker-built machine may well be that aircraft. As such, it was decorated with the *Jasta* 15 colours of a dark blue fuselage and red engine cowling. At the time this photograph was taken, the blue paint extended only as far forward as the mid-point of the cockpit, and the factory finish of streaky olive camouflage is still evident forward of the cockpit to the cowling. It is unknown if further paint was ever applied to complete the colour scheme. The top surfaces of both wings were also dark blue (to identify the machine of the *Geschwader Kommandeur*), and a white panel of unknown significance was displayed on the top wing centre section. Berthold's familiar winged sword insignia decorated both sides of the fuselage. The CO wrote that he could fly the D VII quite easily, even with his crippled right arm, and scored his first claim in the type on 28 May (*HAC/UTD*)

45

Jasta 12 out of action, and *Jasta* 13's effectiveness was also impaired. Furthermore, oil and fuel were in short supply.

The *Geschwader* rarely operated in full strength, and each *Jasta* flew by an operational timetable. While one unit was at the front, another waited in readiness for take-off and one or two were at rest. When numerous enemy formations appeared at once, the airborne *Staffel* would be heavily engaged and other bombers might break though and complete their missions before the reserve units could intercept them.

A primary target for the bombers was the railway junction at St Quentin – the 'life vein' of the 18. *Armee*. It is said the frustrated pilots of *Jasta* 12 could sometimes only stand by 'with clenched teeth' and view these raids from the ground due to the lack of fuel and functional aircraft. Their spirits sank even lower when they received ten Dr Is as replacements instead of D VIIs.

JASTA 15 IN THE ASCENDANT

2 June 1918 was the 24th birthday of *Jasta* 15's Josef Veltjens, and von Ziegesar again left a lively account of this day:

'It is early, 0500 hrs on 2 June 1918 in France. The orderly is just now bringing the wash water in the popular English patrol cans, which we found in heaps at captured English airfields. Drunk with sleep, I ask how the weather is, because last night heavy rain had made the prospects for flying today appear very gloomy. "The early *Staffel* is going, *Herr* Leutnant", was the vague yet completely comprehensible answer. Through the window frames of nailed boards I clearly saw a tiny piece of blue sky floating by. A tender nudge in the ribs of "Seppl" Veltjens snoring beside me on the same mattress on the floor had, for an exception, surprising success in awaking him after only three tries.

'"Hey, Seppl, shall we? Fine weather, and just for your birthday. Come, you already know, etc., etc."

'So, up from the musty mattress, put your skull in the sink and with the virtuosity of a frontline soldier, our preparations were completed in an astonishingly brief time. We had to be quiet so that our comrades, still lying near us in the shot-up houses in Mesnil, noticed nothing – this was due to a terrible oath. This was indeed our *Staffel* leader "Seppl" Veltjens's birthday, and the *Staffel* had secretly decided to "serve him a Tommy" for breakfast as a birthday surprise before he had appeared that morning. They wanted to take off secretly, shoot down at least one and surprise him with this early morning success. However, this plan had reached "Seppl's" ears and it spurred on his own ambitions to spoil this surprise. That's why he had taken me into his confidence.

'As we came onto the airfield, another *Staffel* from our *Geschwader* that had an early take-off today was getting ready to head for the front. This was perfect for us because it wouldn't be obvious when we roared away at the same time. The astonished mechanics quickly took our machines out of the tents and in a few minutes we two were rolling toward the airstrip in our new Fokker D VIIs, which we had acquired only a few days before. "Seppl" raises his hand – full speed – and our thundering blue birds with red "beaks" sweep up into the radiating early morning sunshine.

'Without any trouble, we go to the front. It is the time when the English observation craft and artillery spotters make their morning visits

It would become a tradition in JG II to mark a pilot's significant 'decade' victories (20th, 30th, etc.) with a wreath-bedecked aircraft and photos. However, the occasion for this shot of the D VII flown by Josef Veltjens was the pilot's 24th birthday on 2 June 1918, as declared by the plaque mounted in the bouquet. His eager pilots had planned to surprise the *Staffelführer* with 'an Englishman for breakfast', but Veltjens got wind of the plan and turned the tables on his men by destroying a British RE 8 in company with von Ziegesar before any of them had awakened. The white winged arrow on the fuselage was the personal insignia of Veltjens, and the demarcation line between the red nose and the dark blue fuselage is evident beneath the ammunition chutes for the machine guns (*courtesy J Young*)

to the front and fly at low heights. Soon we can look out over the area – oh my, above the marshes lay a thick fog which was visible stretching itself far into the enemy hinterlands as well. Over there were fewer prospects for "business" than we had hoped for, and flying closely together, we mutually expressed our regrets in sign language understandable only to us.

'I am just searching the sky above us when suddenly near me, and quite clearly, "tack, tack, tack!" "Seppl" had fired his guns, and throttles down his aeroplane – our sign for attack! I thought that he was kidding, but now he is standing his aircraft on its nose and disappears in a wild dive below me. As I immediately follow him, I first see what his eagle eye had recognised long before me – 100 metres beneath us is a large black crate, an English RE which is amusing itself by photographing our new positions that our field artillery had taken up just the previous night. Well, the fun will soon be over for him. He discovers our approach too late to be able to think of rushing away.

'In perfectly flown banks, the enemy pilot and his heavy aeroplane attempts to evade our attack while shots from the observer's machine gun hail around us. "Seppl" is already behind him and, with deep regrets that Tommy didn't even bring a friend along for me, I have to follow our aerial combat rules and remain above Veltjens in order to protect him from surprises from enemy single-seaters, leaving him to do the job alone.

'This did not take long because the pretty banks were no longer of any use in evading "Seppl's" tried and tested flashing gun barrels. I had hardly seen the first threads of smoke from the phosphorus ammunition out of "Seppl's" guns when the enemy aircraft climbed up quite sharply in the air – too sharply to be healthy – and twisting, she spun into the deep.

'Quickly – secure everything above and then after her in great banks in order to see the exact place of impact. Crash! An awful pile of rubble explodes upon impact, and a bright flame shows the place where the two brave opponents found a hero's death. We landed again exactly 20

JOSEF VELTJENS

The son of a factory manager, Josef 'Seppl' Veltjens was born on 2 June 1894 in Geldern, west of Duisberg. He studied mechanical engineering at the Technical University in Charlottenburg, specialising in combustion engines. On 3 August 1914 he joined the *Kaiserin-Augusta-Garde-Regiment* Nr 4 and saw action on the Western Front, then was attached to *Leib-Grenadier Regt* Nr 8 and rose steadily through the ranks.

Following several unsuccessful attempts, Veltjens transferred to the air service and went through pilot's training at Johannisthal in record time. On 10 May 1916 he was posted to F. Fl. Abt. 23, where as an enlisted pilot he performed stellar service in the Battle of the Somme, and first met Joachim von Ziegesar and his mentor Rudolf Berthold. His sterling record earned him a commission in the reserves and training as a fighter pilot. Soon after Berthold was given command

of *Jasta* 14, he arranged for Veltjens to follow him to that unit, where the Rhinelander began practising the trade of a *Jagdflieger*.

Under Berthold's tutelage, Veltjens honed his skills and downed his first confirmed victim in 'Bloody April', with a SPAD credited on the 14th. The next month was a great one, as he added a Farman on 4 May and followed this the next day with a SPAD. Veltjens ended the month with another SPAD on the 31st, and repeated this feat the next day to bring his total to five. He naturally followed Berthold to *Jasta* 18 when the latter became CO on 12 August.

By October Veltjens had reached a tally of eight, but on the 6th the demanding Berthold still wrote in his diary, 'If "Seppl" stays alive then he'll continue to obtain splendid victories. He is like a young hunting dog. He still doesn't get the hang of it, even though he has a very nice number of victories.' Veltjens made the transfer to *Jasta* 15 with the rest of his fellows on 20 March 1918. His scoring rate picked up with three victories in May, and in the same month he was finally entrusted with command of *Jasta* 15 on the 18th. Two days later he received his 'Hohenzollern'. With the advent of the Fokker D VII his tempo increased, and he scored nine times in June. August brought eight more victims, and the 'Blue Max' on the 16th. He led *Jasta* 15 to war's end, with a total of 35 victories.

Like Berthold, Veltjens was an enthusiastic *Freikorps* warrior in the post-war period. He served as an armoured vehicle commander in the Lüttwitz and Gerstenberg *Freikorps*, and was wounded three times in the fighting at Bremen. Then he took up a new life as a merchant sailor with his sailing ship the *Merkur*. Veltjens joined the Nazi party early on, and rose to the rank of colonel in the Luftwaffe in World War 2. On a flight from Milan to Rome on 6 October 1943, his Ju 52/3m transport crashed in the Apennines and he was killed.

---

minutes after we had left the airfield, and with the joking complaints of his comrades who were deprived of their surprise, Veltjens received congratulations for his 15th aerial victory, and his 24th birthday.'

Berthold and the "blue birds" of *Jasta* 15 were doing most of the scoring these days. On 5 June, Berthold downed a DH 9 for his 39th victim north of St Just – another example of the British aircraft JG II was again encountering. 6 June was a stellar day for the *Jasta*, with six victories credited. At about 1110 hrs, the red-nosed D VIIs intercepted a flight of

Ltn d R Josef Veltjens was a loyal disciple of Berthold throughout his career as a fighter pilot, and was rewarded with full command of *Jasta* 15 on 18 May 1918

Another view of a *Jasta* 13 Albatros D V or D Va is provided by this shot of Werner Niethammer's machine being salvaged. The green nose and blue fuselage can be easily seen. Niethammer's personal emblem of a white hammer (Niethammer translates as 'riveting hammer') is just visible on the fuselage aft of the cockpit. The fin and rudder were white. Niethammer was probably flying one of his unit's first D VIIs when he netted a Bréguet on 9 June for his initial victim, and would score five more times flying the Fokker throughout the summer and autumn (*N W O'Connor*)

The first D VIIs for *Jasta* 13 had arrived by 9 June 1918, and one of them may have been this machine. The three bullet hole patches (marked with tricolour cockades) reveal that Uffz Heinrich Piel's Fokker D VII 373/18 had already seen combat by the time this photograph was taken at Les Mesnil in June 1918. Piel was one of three *Jasta* 13 pilots (along with Hencke and Niethammer) who achieved their first victories on 9 June. Piel's early Fokker-built aircraft displayed his personal emblem of a white stork, along with the usual green nose and dark blue fuselage. The white serial number 373 is still visible through the blue overpaint (*J Guttman*)

DH 4s from No 27 Sqn that had just dropped their bombs near Flaby. Nineteen-year-old Georg von Hantelmann and Joachim von Ziegesar were both credited with downing bombers for their first confirmed successes, and von Beaulieu claimed a third (only one DH was actually lost, as two others returned safely with wounded crewmen).

About eight hours later Veltjens, Klein and von Beaulieu each claimed SE 5s. At noon the next day the *Staffel* again tangled with de Havilland bombers, this time from No 49 Sqn. Veltjens and von Beaulieu had successful combats, while Uffz Weischer had one 'forced to land' behind enemy lines. *Jasta* 19 was also in combat, as Rahn claimed an SE 5 (unconfirmed) while Vfw Maschinsky was made a PoW.

Finally enough D VIIs arrived for *Jasta* 13 to be half-equipped with the type, and its month-long dry spell was soon ended in a big way. On 9 June *Staffel* 13 pilots Ernst Hencke, Werner Niethammer and Heinrich Piel each opened their score-sheets, and the veteran Haussmann knocked down a SPAD for his seventh. The resurgent *Jasta* continued making up for lost time on the 10th, as Gefr Willi Laabs destroyed an SE 5 (American 2Lt B Hooper of No 32 Sqn was killed) while the Saxon Franz Büchner destroyed a SPAD to re-enter his name in the victory log after an eight-month interval. Von Hantelmann ensured that *Jasta* 13 would not claim all the glory that day by destroying another SPAD.

Ltn d R Werner Niethammer
acquired his first confirmed claim on
9 June 1918 when he accounted for a
Bréguet 14 near Ribécourt. His
Fokker D VIIs bore his usual emblem
of a white hammer

This less than brilliant photograph
serves to illustrate Niethammer's
individual insignia on his first *Jasta*
13 D VII. This was an early Fokker-
built example, and the crosses on
the wings bear evidence of
conversion from an earlier form. The
unusual rudder cross is noteworthy

The success enjoyed by JG II in June indicates that Berthold's uncompromising discipline was paying off, but it was at a high price to the *Kommandeur* and his pilots. He emphatically hammered his sense of duty and discipline into the young airmen. He later wrote, 'I had great difficulties with them until I brought them up to a high level of flying skill, and until I grew fond of them. I am attached to every single one. But do the people feel it? I don't think so. They always only feel the severity.' In reality, he rarely breathed a word of praise to his men. His formula for combat was attack the enemy as closely as possible, at the lowest possible height, and using as little ammunition as possible.

One of Berthold's pilots in *Jasta* 18 was the 14-victory ace Paul Strähle, who recalled that Berthold had three golden rules when it came to his pilots leaving patrols with various excuses.

'*Abbiegen kenne ich nicht, Motordefekte kenne ich nicht, Munition ausgegangen kenne ich nicht!*' Roughly translated, it means 'I won't have any turning away, I won't have any engine trouble and I won't have any running out of ammunition around here!' If a pilot's guns jammed, he had to stick around – the enemy could not know, and was more afraid of someone who did not waste their ammunition at long range. Von Ziegesar recalled, 'Berthold demanded performances from us that appeared prodigious, yet he was always the first to carry them out. His principle was always, "We are not here to carry out a 'gentlemanly' combat at 5000 metres – the infantry at the front is expecting us, and we have to help them."'

On 10 June the *Geschwader* made 73 front flights, and 76 the next day when *Jasta* 13 downed four victims, including the firsts for Uffz Walter Hertsch and Ltn d R Kurt Hetze. In addition, *Jasta* 15 accounted for three British aircraft, two of them going to Veltjens to bring his tally to the significant 20 mark. The next day, JG II performed 66 front flights. In spite of such efforts, the effectiveness of half of the *Geschwader* remained seriously compromised by faulty equipment. By mid-June, *Jasta* 19 had only a partial complement of D VIIs and *Jasta* 12 was still totally equipped with triplanes. With fuel and oil becoming (*text continues on page 65*)

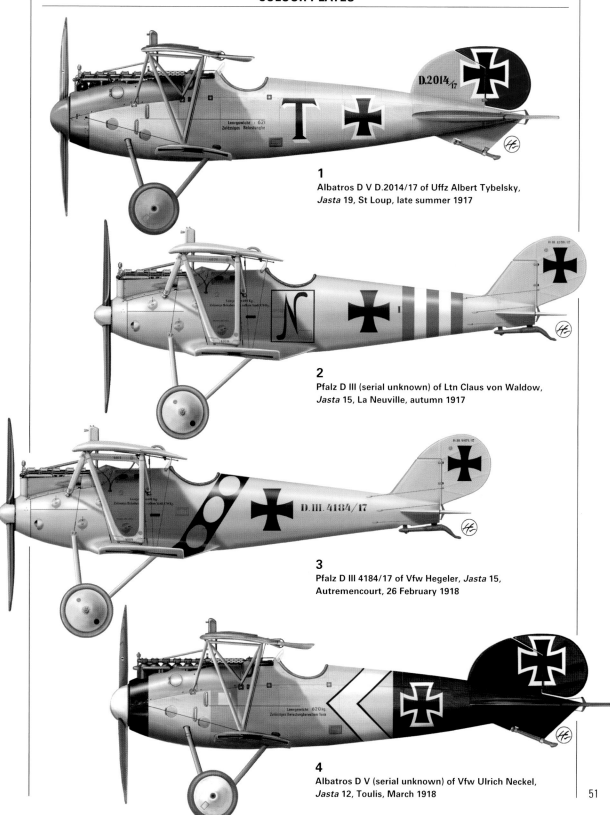

1
Albatros D V D.2014/17 of Uffz Albert Tybelsky,
Jasta 19, St Loup, late summer 1917

2
Pfalz D III (serial unknown) of Ltn Claus von Waldow,
Jasta 15, La Neuville, autumn 1917

3
Pfalz D III 4184/17 of Vfw Hegeler, *Jasta* 15,
Autremencourt, 26 February 1918

4
Albatros D V (serial unknown) of Vfw Ulrich Neckel,
Jasta 12, Toulis, March 1918

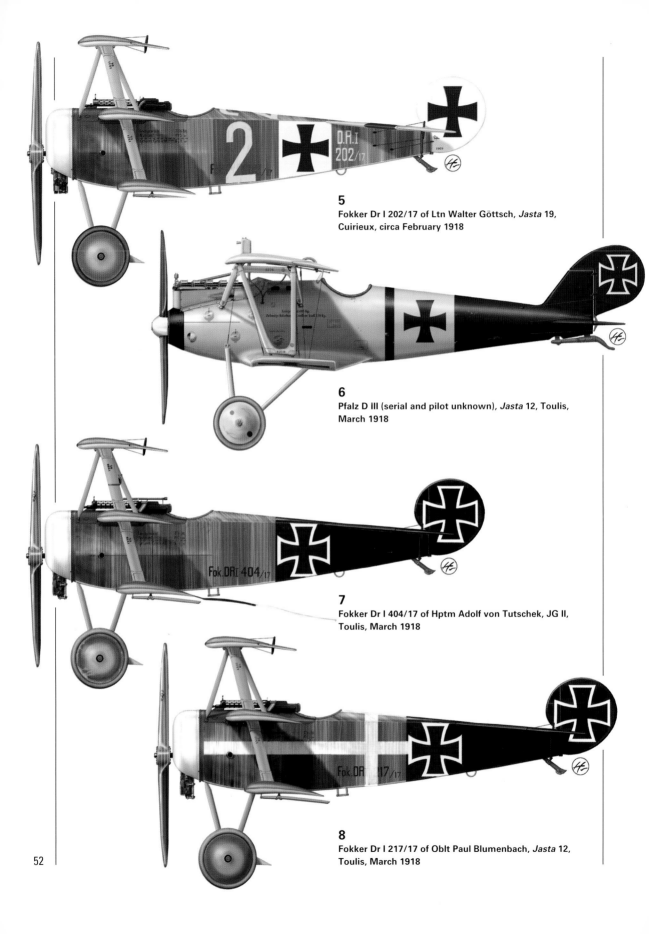

5
Fokker Dr I 202/17 of Ltn Walter Göttsch, *Jasta* 19,
Cuirieux, circa February 1918

6
Pfalz D III (serial and pilot unknown), *Jasta* 12, Toulis,
March 1918

7
Fokker Dr I 404/17 of Hptm Adolf von Tutschek, JG II,
Toulis, March 1918

8
Fokker Dr I 217/17 of Oblt Paul Blumenbach, *Jasta* 12,
Toulis, March 1918

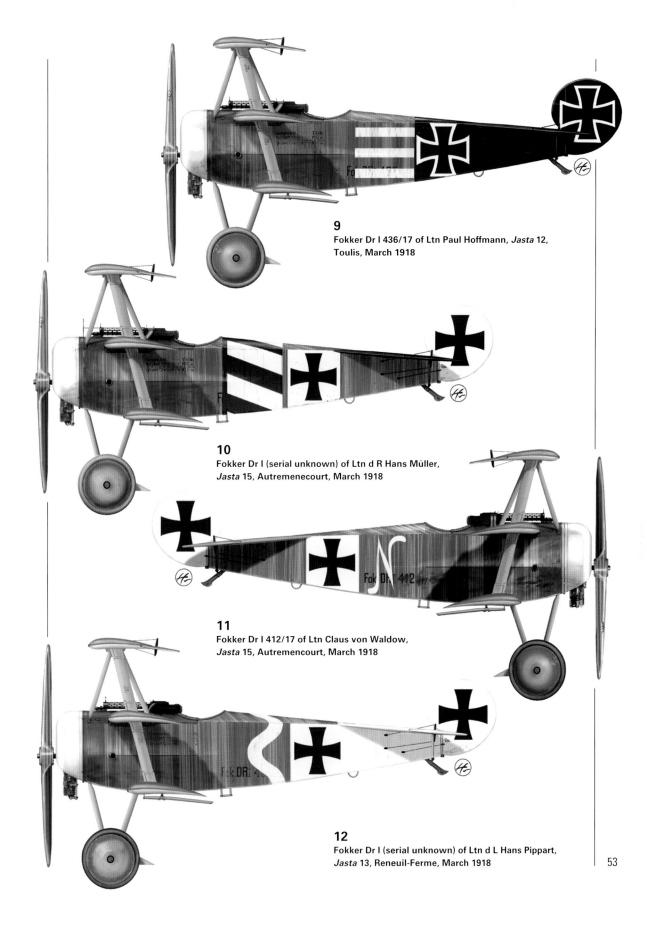

9
Fokker Dr I 436/17 of Ltn Paul Hoffmann, *Jasta* 12,
Toulis, March 1918

10
Fokker Dr I (serial unknown) of Ltn d R Hans Müller,
Jasta 15, Autremenecourt, March 1918

11
Fokker Dr I 412/17 of Ltn Claus von Waldow,
Jasta 15, Autremencourt, March 1918

12
Fokker Dr I (serial unknown) of Ltn d L Hans Pippart,
Jasta 13, Reneuil-Ferme, March 1918

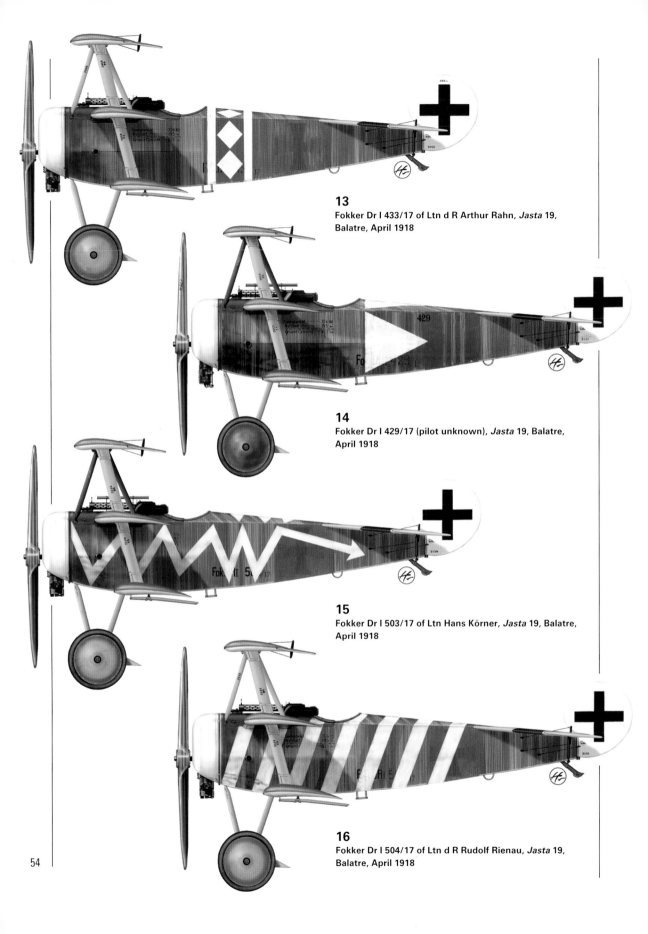

13
Fokker Dr I 433/17 of Ltn d R Arthur Rahn, *Jasta* 19,
Balatre, April 1918

14
Fokker Dr I 429/17 (pilot unknown), *Jasta* 19, Balatre,
April 1918

15
Fokker Dr I 503/17 of Ltn Hans Körner, *Jasta* 19, Balatre,
April 1918

16
Fokker Dr I 504/17 of Ltn d R Rudolf Rienau, *Jasta* 19,
Balatre, April 1918

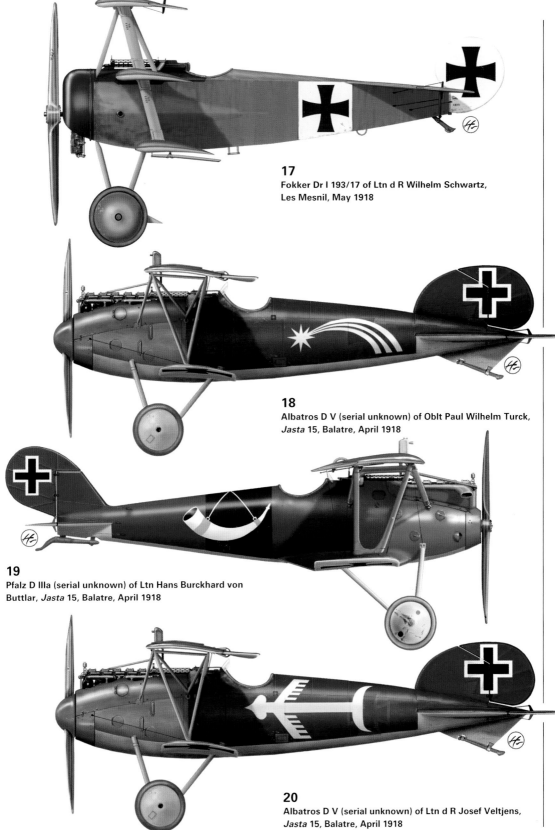

17
Fokker Dr I 193/17 of Ltn d R Wilhelm Schwartz,
Les Mesnil, May 1918

18
Albatros D V (serial unknown) of Oblt Paul Wilhelm Turck,
Jasta 15, Balatre, April 1918

19
Pfalz D IIIa (serial unknown) of Ltn Hans Burckhard von
Buttlar, *Jasta* 15, Balatre, April 1918

20
Albatros D V (serial unknown) of Ltn d R Josef Veltjens,
Jasta 15, Balatre, April 1918

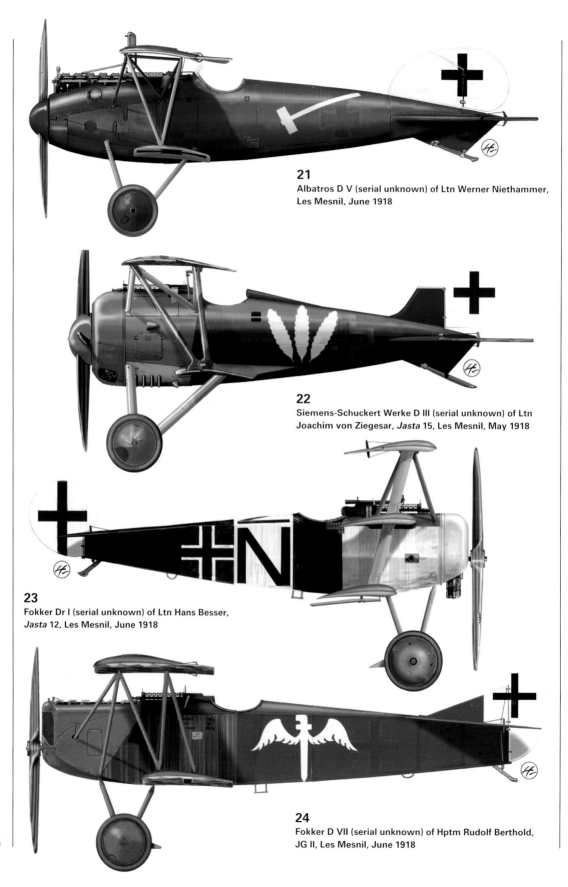

21
Albatros D V (serial unknown) of Ltn Werner Niethammer,
Les Mesnil, June 1918

22
Siemens-Schuckert Werke D III (serial unknown) of Ltn
Joachim von Ziegesar, *Jasta* 15, Les Mesnil, May 1918

23
Fokker Dr I (serial unknown) of Ltn Hans Besser,
Jasta 12, Les Mesnil, June 1918

24
Fokker D VII (serial unknown) of Hptm Rudolf Berthold,
JG II, Les Mesnil, June 1918

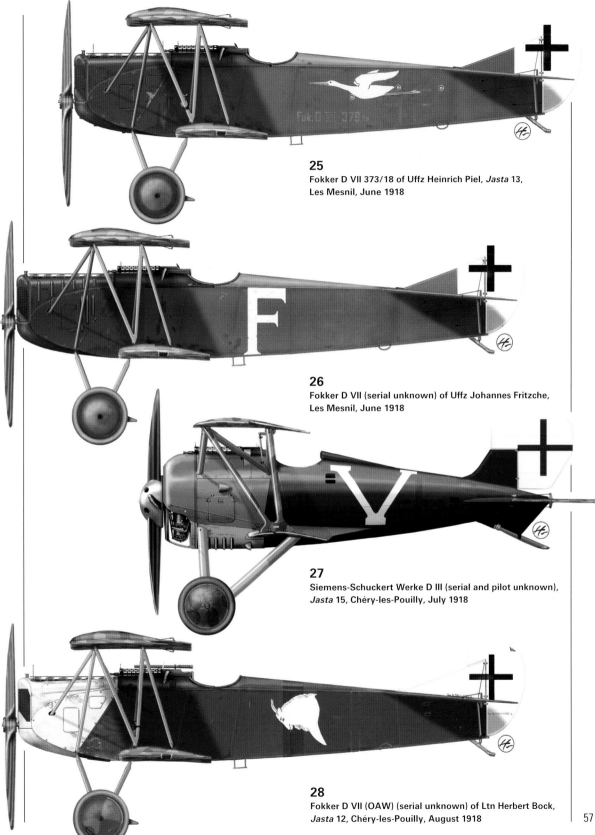

25
Fokker D VII 373/18 of Uffz Heinrich Piel, *Jasta* 13,
Les Mesnil, June 1918

26
Fokker D VII (serial unknown) of Uffz Johannes Fritzche,
Les Mesnil, June 1918

27
Siemens-Schuckert Werke D III (serial and pilot unknown),
Jasta 15, Chéry-les-Pouilly, July 1918

28
Fokker D VII (OAW) (serial unknown) of Ltn Herbert Bock,
Jasta 12, Chéry-les-Pouilly, August 1918

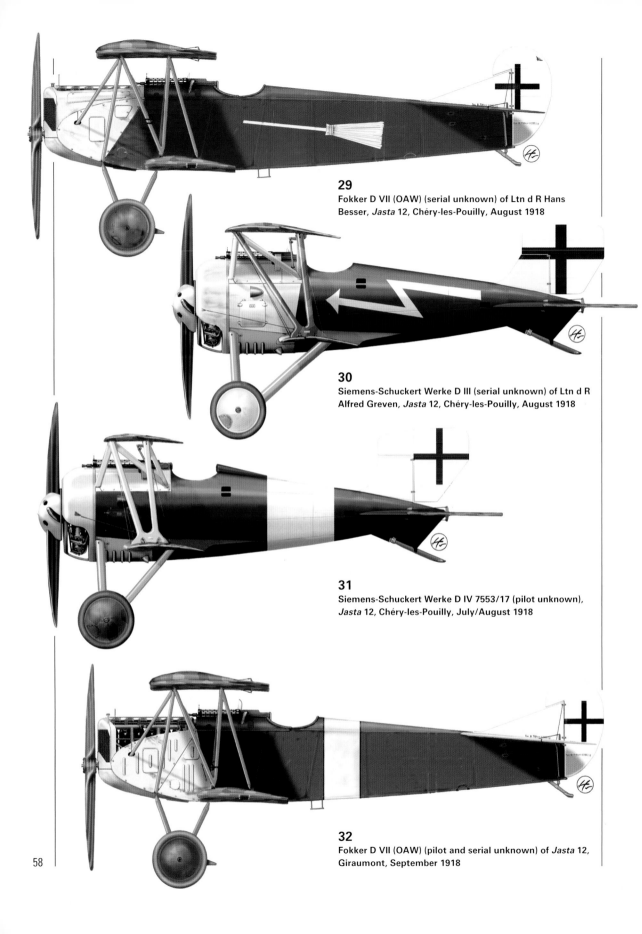

29
Fokker D VII (OAW) (serial unknown) of Ltn d R Hans
Besser, *Jasta* 12, Chéry-les-Pouilly, August 1918

30
Siemens-Schuckert Werke D III (serial unknown) of Ltn d R
Alfred Greven, *Jasta* 12, Chéry-les-Pouilly, August 1918

31
Siemens-Schuckert Werke D IV 7553/17 (pilot unknown),
Jasta 12, Chéry-les-Pouilly, July/August 1918

32
Fokker D VII (OAW) (pilot and serial unknown) of *Jasta* 12,
Giraumont, September 1918

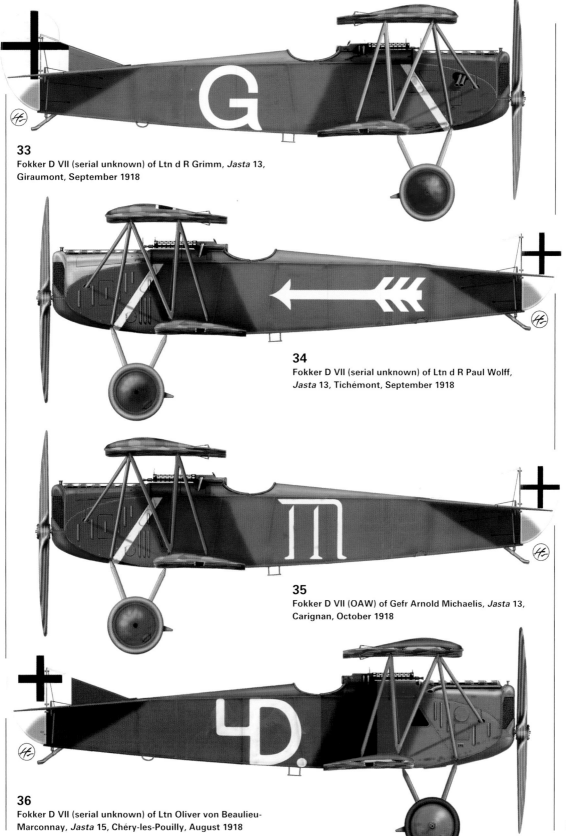

33
Fokker D VII (serial unknown) of Ltn d R Grimm, *Jasta* 13,
Giraumont, September 1918

34
Fokker D VII (serial unknown) of Ltn d R Paul Wolff,
Jasta 13, Tichémont, September 1918

35
Fokker D VII (OAW) of Gefr Arnold Michaelis, *Jasta* 13,
Carignan, October 1918

36
Fokker D VII (serial unknown) of Ltn Oliver von Beaulieu-
Marconnay, *Jasta* 15, Chéry-les-Pouilly, August 1918

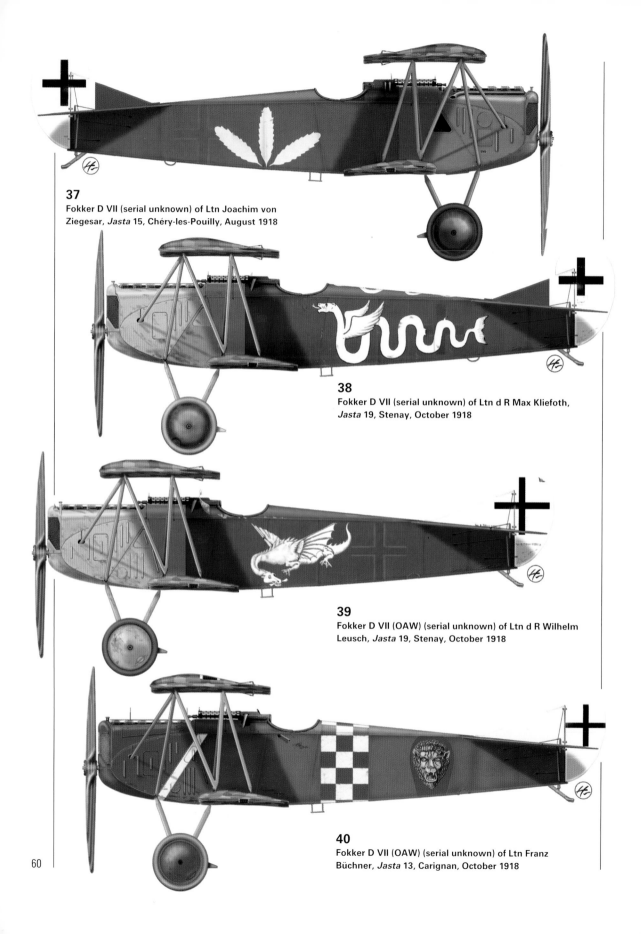

37
Fokker D VII (serial unknown) of Ltn Joachim von
Ziegesar, *Jasta* 15, Chéry-les-Pouilly, August 1918

38
Fokker D VII (serial unknown) of Ltn d R Max Kliefoth,
Jasta 19, Stenay, October 1918

39
Fokker D VII (OAW) (serial unknown) of Ltn d R Wilhelm
Leusch, *Jasta* 19, Stenay, October 1918

40
Fokker D VII (OAW) (serial unknown) of Ltn Franz
Büchner, *Jasta* 13, Carignan, October 1918

10

23

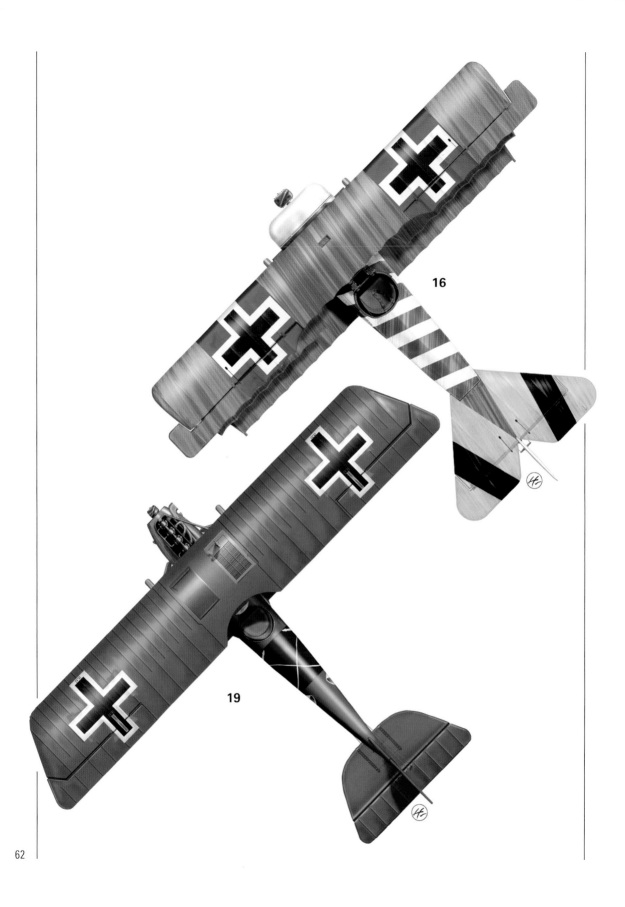

16

19

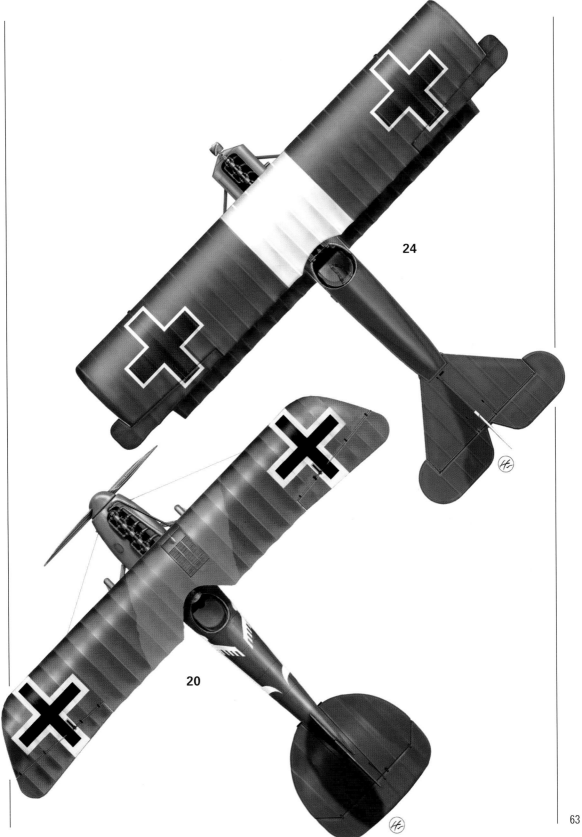

24

20

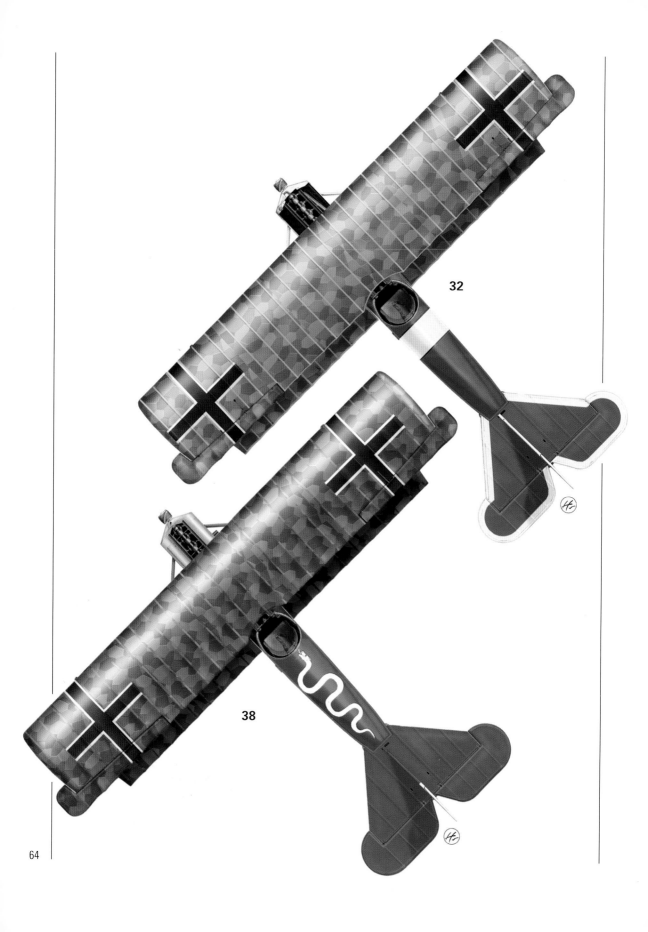

32

38

Nine days after his 24th birthday, Veltjens had another reason to celebrate when his score reached 20 on 11 June. The custom of decorating a pilot's D VII to commemorate his 20th victory was followed on this occasion, and the *Jasta* 15 pilots pose with their commander. The first pilot at extreme left is unidentified, but the rest are, from left, Hugo Schäfer, Georg von Hantelmann (note the death's head cap badge), Veltjens directly under the nose of his D VII, then (probably) Johannes Klein, von Beaulieu-Marconnay and Theodor Weischer. Veltjens' German shepherd dog 'Bella' is trying to wander out of the picture frame at right. The six named pilots here would account for over 120 enemy aircraft by war's end (*N W O'Connor*)

increasingly scarce, it was realised that these vital commodities were far better employed in the D VIIs than in the Dr Is. On 12 June the war diary reported that, 'The Fokker triplanes can no longer be regarded as serviceable for the front.'

The 12th was one of the more eventful days in the *Geschwader* history, as related by von Ziegesar:

'The frontlines, after the advance, had again stalemated, and had created the famous bulge near Montdidier. The Berthold *Geschwader* lay in the middle of this bulge, at the airfield near Mesnil. 12 June now appeared to be the long-awaited day on which the French would attempt a breakthrough from the south toward the north, coming from the direction of Compiegne.

'Up until around midday, the weather was still more or less good. In the late morning, during a flight to the front, Veltjens, Beaulieu and Hantelmann were successful in shooting down two SE 5s and two Bréguets. When rain set in at midday, we already began regretting spending the rest of the day – which had begun so promisingly – doing nothing, particularly when the ever-increasing rumble of artillery fire showed us that "something was happening up there".

'In a vague and unpleasant mood, we seven pilots of the Berthold *Staffel* sit in our so-called *Kasino* in Mesnil. Outside it's begun to rain fiercely.

While *Jasta* 15 had a full complement of Fokker D VIIs by the beginning of June, the other *Staffeln* had to carry on flying the worn-out Fokker triplanes and even Albatros machines for a bit longer. This splendid study shows Ltn d R Kurt Hetze with his *Jasta* 13 Albatros D Va, apparently in early June 1918. The early thick form of *Balkenkreuz* insignia is discernible on the wing undersides and tail, and the machine displays the *Staffel* 13 colours instituted by Berthold – a green nose and dark blue fuselage and tailplane. The fin and rudder were painted white in concordance with the 17 March 1918 directive. Hetze achieved his first victory on 11 June when he destroyed the SPAD XIII flown by the commander of SPA94, Lt de La Rochfordière, at 1200 hrs (*courtesy Helge K – Werner Dittmann*)

Conversation cannot be made. Even the mouth of von Beaulieu, which normally never stops, is silent. Damn this inactivity.

'It was already approaching six o'clock when, suddenly, in the door, Berthold. "Get ready, *meine Herren.* The *Staffel* takes off in ten minutes. I will lead. At the front, north-west of Noyon, French bombers are smashing our artillery and infantry columns to pieces, and we sit here drinking coffee. The weather at the front is somewhat better. If the *Staffel* is separated, everyone will attack individually. I don't need to tell my *Staffel* that each one of you must stay at the front until the last drop of petrol. Advancing enemy on the ground is also a worthy target."

'All of us had to jump up and rush out of the building. Through the splashing mud of the torn-up village street to the nearby airfield. Already the mechanics are pushing the otherwise well-protected new Fokkers into the falling summer rain.

'While we are dressing, a glance at the sky. Well, what about it – are the clouds as high as 200 metres? It doesn't matter. Up front our bravest are waiting and the enemy can torture them unhindered. The *Staffel* is already gathering and, splattering mud, the first aircraft are lifting up, closely followed by the others. The raindrops glide in light threads from the blue wings and cloud our goggle lenses. At a height of 100 metres, the eight blue birds fly towards the front to our beleaguered comrades-in-arms on the ground. Soon our eyes, well accustomed to the front, see the flaring muzzle flashes of our artillery out of the midst of spraying clouds of earth from the enemy's shots.

'150 metres – the edge of the clouds. Something is darting about over there. There appears to be many of them. The usual drill-like tight formation of the *Staffel* has shattered in the shreds of cloud which we had flown through. Diving out of the cloudy haze, I see under me the winged sword, Berthold, fighting with a French infantry aircraft. Stay near him? No, no reason. Give cover up above. Already it is crackling and thudding. To the right and left of me are cockades, at close range. Full speed, into a bank and fire at the opponent on the left. He is gone in the clouds.

'Continue flying. Where am I? Gaze downwards. There – a gray-blue column is moving out of a trench. Ah, French! Glance upward, cut the petrol, stick forward and my good machine guns rattle agreeably. I see how the enemy infantry throw themselves down, run away from each other. Full throttle, up! There – my breath failed – not 100 metres above me, cockades upon cockades, an entire squadron coming towards me. There is no time to count, as already the eager little glowworms of the enemy are whizzing around me. Now, calmness and confidence, pull back on the throttle, pick one out from the plump group, pull up, calmly aim and out with a burst. My opponent falls under me like a stone, goes into a left bank and smashes to pieces at the edge of a forest.

'During this series of events, two blue Fokkers dive closely past me, which I recognise as Berthold and Schäfer. After them. Still in a bank, I see Schäfer's steeply climbing aeroplane, and simultaneously in front of him, a burning aircraft crashing down to the earth out of a mass of French bombers. But where has Berthold gone? Only after we have rejoined each other do we discover him far on the other side of the lines. The enemy squadron is not out of sight. We fly over to Berthold who, at the lowest height, is pushing an opponent from behind further into enemy territory.

'The battle's front area lies behind us. Again, the rain is hitting our faces. Berthold is sitting doggedly behind his opponent. Our instruments indicate 200 kilometres per hour – the extreme limit. Then the enemy fighter – just as we recognised him as such – rushes at full throttle into a row of trees and burns! Berthold makes a turn and waves at us as we hook up with him. Where are we? Street, forest, village – everything is unfamiliar. No shell craters. We must be far behind the lines. At a height of 50 metres, we roar behind Berthold. There – marching troops – we have the direction. Berthold dives down, we follow right behind. We clearly observe the effects of our bursts as the marching column is torn asunder.

'One hour has gone by since our take-off. We have petrol for one hour and 20 minutes! Now to home. We three fly towards the soon recognisable front. From below one clearly hears the barking of artillery and machine guns, while flak only mildly pesters us. One continuously steals glances at the indicator on the petrol gauge. We are over the front.

'Suddenly a cockade-carrier dives out of the clouds in front of us with hammering machine guns. Berthold is already behind him. I see how his phosphorus lines follow him into the sheltering clouds. Berthold, too, has disappeared into the haze.

'Only ten minutes of petrol!

'We console ourselves that Berthold will soon come along. We find our directions again and Schäfer and I land at our airfield with empty tanks. Happy with our successes, we are again sitting in our mess. On this day, Veltjens had downed his 21st and 22nd opponents, and due to this was definitely ready for the *Pour le Mérite*. Beaulieu had shot down his sixth, Hantelmann his 3rd and 4th, Schäfer his 4th. And Berthold – where was the old Franconian? Requests at neighbouring airfields and observation posts at the front are unsuccessful.

'We sit awake for a long time. All possibilities are tried repeatedly and long-distance telephone messages sent. Finally, in the morning hours, a furious call comes in. On this flight Hptm Berthold had shot down the third opponent, and he himself had landed in the frontlines of our forward infantry with an empty tank and a shot-up aircraft. He directed that a new aeroplane should be immediately readied for early morning and a truck should pick him up there, near a howitzer battery. *That* was Berthold.'

In spite of von Ziegesar's statement, Berthold received confirmation for only one victim (a SPAD) on 12 June. All the same, Berthold and his *Jasta* 15 worthies chalked up seven aircraft destroyed, and Pippart added another SE 5, for the loss of Ltn d R Hugo Schulz of *Jasta* 12. The next day Berthold wrote:

'Yesterday my motor was shot up. In the last few days the boys (the enemy pilots) have really taken me to the cleaners. There are just simply too many. I picked out my opponent of yesterday from 100 enemy aircraft. That was a neat battle. Veltjens did well for himself.'

The endeavours of *Jasta* 15 in these frenetic days did not go unnoticed, for the daily report of the *Kofl* of the 18. *Armee* stated:

'Extract from a report of *Schlachtstaffelgruppe* 3 of 11 June 1918. A *Fokkerstaffel* with red fronts, which worked far over the enemy lines above the *Geschwader,* energetically participated in the defence against enemy aerial forces. I am glad to be able to report this beautiful cooperation over enemy lines to all aerial forces.'

It was 'officers only' for this convivial grouping of the young *Leutnante* of *Jasta* 13 in the first half of June 1918. They are, from the left, Ernst Hencke, *Staffelführer* Wilhelm Schwartz, Ulrich Neckel, Franz Büchner, Werner Niethammer and Kurt Hetze. After his sixth victory, Schwartz was badly wounded during a balloon attack on 15 June and left the *Staffel* (although he would survive and take over *Jasta* 73 in October). This led to Büchner taking command of the unit, and together with Neckel he would bring the *Jasta* to a high level of proficiency
(*Helge K – Werner Dittmann*)

The young *Pour le Mérite* ace Kurt Wüsthoff arrived at JG II on 16 June 1918, but was shot down and taken prisoner the very next day on only his second flight with *Jasta* 15. He had 27 victories, but had been posted out of JG I under rather dubious circumstances due to shattered nerves and conflicts with his men. Although he survived his serious leg wounds and lengthy French imprisonment, he died following an aircraft crash in 1926

Jasta 13 was also successful. On 14 June the *Staffel* engaged Camels from No 80 Sqn over Dreslincourt at around 2010 hrs, and commander Wilhelm Schwartz gained his sixth victory, while Neckel achieved a double to raise his tally to 12. It was Schwartz's last hurrah, for the next day he was badly wounded in the upper arm during a balloon attack. His replacement was the incipient *Kanone* Franz Büchner, with a long record of service in the unit and four victories – a new era was beginning in *Jasta* 13. That day the 18. *Armee Kofl* report praised the successes of *Staffeln* 13 and 15, but also brought the depressing news that every *Jasta* would be rationed to just 14,000 litres of fuel and 4000 litres of oil per month.

At 0955 hrs on 16 June a flight of DH 4s and DH 9s of No 27 Sqn took off on a bombing raid, but five would not return. A few miles west of Roye they were apparently bounced by the 'red-noses' of *Jasta* 15, although it is slightly possible *Jasta* Boelcke was also involved. Four of the de Havillands were lost with their crews (one falling in flames) and another limped back with a wounded crew, the pilot later dying of his wounds. Veltjens, Schäfer, von Beaulieu and Klein each claimed one of the bombers, and Uffz Weischer gained his first confirmed victim from the day's carnage.

Schäfer's day was not an unqualified success, as he also tangled with a very well-flown SE 5. During the scrap he heard a loud bang under the cowling, the revs dropped and suddenly he had a dead engine at low altitude far over the enemy lines. Luckily for him his opponent didn't notice this – Schäfer's D VII took a beating from Allied ground fire as he glided back across the lines. Managing a landing just behind the German trenches, he wrote off his Fokker but survived to fight another day.

ACES FALL

16 June also saw a new face on the JG II staff, although a well-known one. Ltn d R Kurt Wüsthoff, former commander of *Jasta* 4, had won the *Pour le Mérite* at the age of 19, and had 27 confirmed victories. He had been posted out of JG I and had just spent time recuperating from gastric ailments and a 'nervous disorder' prior to arriving at JG II. On 17 June he borrowed von Hantelmann's D VII 382/18 and flew in a *Jasta* 15 patrol under Berthold's leadership. What happened next is explained in a letter from Berthold to Wüsthoff's mother, providing a rare glimpse of a compassionate side of the *Kommandeur*:

'Dear Madam,

'As you, dear Madam, have already been informed, your son did not return from a combat flight one week ago. I express my sincere sympathies to you that you had to lose your son so quickly after he had just returned from his family to the front.

'I had taken him into the *Staffel* of my *Geschwader* with which I always fly. Thus we were flying together – it was the second combat patrol for him in the *Geschwader* – on 17 June as well.

'On the other side of the front we got into a fight with enemy single-seater fighters which were hotly attacked by him right at the beginning. The men of my *Staffel* quickly helped him out, but straightaway – due to the greater numbers of the enemy – it was no longer possible for one to look out for the other because now one was himself busy with an opponent.

'When the *Staffel* gathered together again after the aerial battle, your son was missing. He was not seen crashing, rather going down to the ground in spirals on the other side. Upon this, I immediately ordered that requests be made of the opponent concerning his whereabouts, but with the current state of fighting, and the way in which the war has intensified because of its length, the prospects of an answer are slim.

'In spite of this, however, if I should be able to learn anything about your son, then I will, my dear madam, have the news promptly sent to you. In the meantime, I once again ensure you of my condolences. I remain yours,

'Berthold.'

Georg von Hantelmann's *Jasta* 15 Fokker D VII 382/18 was being flown by Kurt Wüsthoff when the latter pilot was brought down by pilots of No 24 Sqn on 17 June 1918. Here is the Fokker's fuselage on its way to No 24 Sqn's airfield at Conteville. The skull and crossbones emblem on the blue fuselage was a reference to von Hantelmann's former service in the *Husaren-Regiment* Nr 17, a 'death's head' regiment from Brunswick (*via S K Taylor*)

Proud of their action in capturing Wüsthoff, the personnel of No 24 Sqn fashioned a unique trophy from the Fokker D VII 382/18 he was flying. The fin and rudder have been made into a wind vane and adornment for the squadron notice board, mounted outside the CO's office at Conteville. A small replica of the death's head insignia was created to balance the wind vane (*via S K Taylor*)

Jasta 15 had attacked 13 SE 5 fighters – all three flights – of No 24 Sqn, with many experienced RAF pilots among them. 2Lt John H Southey later related that he had picked out one of the Fokkers and put a burst from both guns into it with a full deflection shot. The D VII went down in a series of half rolls, and Southey could not follow it. When he returned he learned that Capts MacDonald, Johnson and Lt Barton had apparently followed the Fokker D VII down, which crashed inside the French lines.

The blue Fokker with the skull and crossbones insignia was brought to the squadron's aerodrome at Conteville. Several pilots from No 24 visited Wüsthoff in the hospital, and he told them that the first SE 5 to fire on him (Southey) had wounded him. Nonetheless, MacDonald, Johnson and Barton attained official credit, and even Dolphin pilot C E Walton of No 23 Sqn put in a claim.

The Allies lost an ace of their own at the hands of JG II the evening of that very same 17 June. Three SPADs from the celebrated *Escadrille* SPA3 (the *Cigognes*) were on patrol between Orvillers and Rollot. They were flown by MdL Dubonnet and Sgt Macari, under the leadership of American Sgt Frank Baylies, a highly decorated flier with 12 victories. According to French accounts, they encountered a group of unfamiliar aircraft over Montdidier, and Baylies led the flight up towards them to investigate. Suddenly Baylies wheeled over on one wing as he recognised them as Fokker triplanes.

The Dr Is were flown by four *Jasta* 19 pilots, among them Wilhelm Leusch and Rudolf Rienau, who succeeded in wringing the most out of their old triplanes. In the swirling combat Baylies was shot down in flames before his comrades could assist him, and Dubonnet somehow managed to bring his riddled SPAD to a crash landing within French lines. The SPADs were credited to Leusch and Rienau as the second victory for each.

Berthold continued driving himself and his men to their limit. Despite hazy afternoon skies, the *Geschwader* made 56 front flights on the 18th and fought numerous combats. The two young friends of *Jasta* 15, von Hantelmann and von Beaulieu, furthered their friendly scoring competition as both downed fighters. Their grimly fanatical *Kommandeur* continued to ignore his injuries to destroy two SE 5s from No 84 Sqn. The next day Berthold wrote:

Jagdstaffel 19's pilots retained their Fokker triplanes well into June 1918, no doubt eagerly anticipating D VIIs. *Staffel* commander Hans Pippart is seventh from left in this photograph of the *Jasta's* aircrew, perhaps taken in May. In the background is the top wing of Pippart's Dr I 471/17, with his disc emblem just discernible on the centre section on the original print. Fourth from left in this group, almost hidden, is Arthur Rahn, while sixth from left, to the right of Pippart, is thought to be Wilhelm Leusch. Tenth from left, in the rear, is Hans Körner and just next to him (11th from left) is probably Rudolf Rienau. On 17 June Leusch and Rienau, apparently in one of the last successful triplane actions of *Jasta* 19, downed Sgt Frank Baylies and MdL Dubonnet of SPA 3 (*via N W O'Connor*)

Ltn d L Hans Pippart, leader of *Jasta* 19, poses with a Dr I from his unit – possibly his own 471/17. He served as *Staffelführer* of the unit from 19 April 1918 until his death on 11 August

Jasta 12 was the last *Staffel* in JG II still to be completely equipped with the Fokker Dr I in mid June 1918. By then the unit's effectiveness was seriously compromised by the unserviceability of its equipment. Here are nine of the unit's last triplanes, seen at Les Mesnil shortly before they were finally retired on 24 June. By this time the motley collection of Dr Is included some that had been handed over from other *Staffeln*. On some of them, the initial black tail unit markings have been supplemented by additional black(?) and white markings along the length of the fuselage, and all of the Dr Is display a worn and dirtied appearance. Fourth from the left is the chequerboard-marked machine which some have attributed to Becker, and next is the 'N' marked Dr I flown by Hans Besser (*courtesy A Imrie*)

'It's raining today. Thank God, because otherwise it would have been impossible for me to fly with the others. My arm has gotten worse. It is rather swollen and infected underneath the open wound. I believe the bone splinters are forcibly pushing themselves out because the swollen area is very hard. The pain is terrific. During my air battle yesterday, during which I shot down two English single-seaters in flames for my 35th and 36th victories, I screamed out loud from the pain. All the swelling came since last night. Why couldn't it have come earlier?'

Just as troubling to Berthold were his continuing problems with equipment. The war diary entry for 19 June concluded that *Jagdstaffeln* 12 and 19 had no serviceable aircraft, thus taking half of the group out of action. In the next few days JG II finally received enough D VIIs to entirely equip *Jasta* 13 and half of *Jasta* 19. *Jasta* 12 received the other

Vfw Albert Haussmann had achieved six victories before being posted to *Jasta* 13. Once he received the Fokker D VII his scoring rate intensified, as it did with so many others. He poses here with his Fokker-built D VII that displayed the green nose and dark blue fuselage of *Staffel* 13. Haussmann's personal insignia was the two-colour 'engrailed' fuselage band. In July he survived a collision with another Fokker, suffering only minor head injuries (*Dr V Koos via P Grosz*)

When *Jasta* 19 finally replaced its triplanes with D VIIs, some of its Dr Is apparently went to *Jasta* 12. This aeroplane is believed to be Dr I 471/17, formerly flown by Hans Pippart – his disc insignia can still be seen on the fuselage sides and deck. However, much of the fuselage and tail was painted over, and the final style of national insignia has been repainted on the fuselage and in the outboard position on the wings. Furthermore, the tailplane and elevators have been painted a solid dark colour with a white chevron. It is believed this aircraft was in *Jasta* 12 service when this photograph was taken, probably at Les Mesnil in June. The pilot at the extreme right is Franz Büchner of *Jasta* 13, and to the left of him is Oblt Walter Dingel, technical officer for JG II (*Helge K – Werner Dittmann*)

units' cast-off triplanes, but on 24 June *Kofl* deemed the Fokker Dr I unfit for further duty. All the *Geschwader* triplanes were ferried to the *Armee Flug Park* 18, leaving *Jasta* 12 totally ineffective – the unit had four leftover Siemens fighters, but these were 'unfit for the front' as well.

It fell to the D VII pilots of *Jagdstaffeln* 13 and 15 to carry the burden of combat, and they did so with ardour on 25 June, netting six enemy aircraft. At noon, south of Albert, Franz Büchner led the green-nosed D VIIs of *Jasta* 13 into a scrap with Bristol fighters of the formidable No 48 Sqn at a height of 5000 metres. Neckel raised his tally to 16 with two Bristols destroyed. Kurt Hetze doggedly pursued another F2B in spite of his jammed right-hand gun, spattering the two-seater with bursts from his one functioning weapon. He scored telling hits in the engine area and the F2B went down.

Hetze then went after a Bristol that was attacking Vfw Albert Haussmann, who had previously served in *Jasta* 15 prior to recently joining *Jasta* 13. Hetze chased it far over the lines at low altitude but failed to bring it down. With Büchner and Haussmann, Hetze pursued a third enemy until he was 500 metres over Amiens, returning through a hail of ground fire that punctured his reserve fuel line. The British flight leader Capt F C Ransley attacked a Fokker apparently flown by Ltn d R Fritz Hillberger, an inexperienced pilot who had just arrived at the *Jasta* three days earlier. Ransley fired from close range, nearly ramming the German, but saw the Fokker break up and fall away in flames. Walter Hertsch of *Jasta* 13 was also severely wounded by the 'Brisfits'. He managed to land at the *Jasta* 28 field, but died of his wounds the next day.

Later on the 25th *Jasta* 15 attacked French bomber formations at about 1850 hrs with their usual deadly efficiency, and Bréguets fell to Veltjens, von Hantelmann and Ltn d R Hans Joachim Borck (his first). Kurt Hetze

One of the weary Fokker triplanes photographed at Les Mesnil in June was this Dr I, seen with Ltn d R Hans Besser in the cockpit. On this machine, further black and white décor had been added forward of the black tail unit marking, and a personal emblem of a black 'N' was marked aft of the cockpit. The significance of this insignia remains unknown. A Morrell airspeed indicator is affixed to the interplane strut, and a tubular sight, rear-view mirror and a rack for flare cartridges were fitted. Late style, full-chord *Balkenkreuz* form insignia were applied to the wings (*courtesy A Imrie*)

seemed to be leading a charmed life, for on the 26th he landed from a flight to discover that the whole of the fabric covering of his top wing had loosened and nearly torn away.

Every evening now seemed to bring on a massive dogfight over the Chemin des Dames, as large formations of French and British fighters flew over the lines. In the 18. *Armee* such an encounter was sardonically called a 'rendezvous of the upper class'. On 27 June the skies over Villers-Brettoneux witnessed a rematch between JG II and No 48 Sqn, as a combined flight from *Staffeln* 13 and 15 clashed with ten Bristols at 1900 hrs.

The RAF group came out badly, losing two crews killed in the action. Haussmann opened his *Jasta* 13 tally with his eighth victory, and Neckel achieved two more to bring his meteoric streak to 18 (with dreams of the *Pour le Mérite* certainly in mind). *Kommandeur* Berthold again showed how it was done with a Bristol sent down in flames. With his total at 37, Berthold was now the ranking living German ace (Udet was next with 35), but he refused to take a well-earned leave, or rest on his laurels:

'Yesterday, I flew again, and shot my 37th down in flames. My arm is still not good. Since the lower wound has broken open again, the pain has diminished somewhat and the swelling has shrunken. Since being wounded I have not had the time to bring my body up to its former capability for resistance – the war, of course, has extremely weakened me. But I must persevere no matter what it costs. After the war we can slowly bring these old bones back into order again.'

Berthold would, indeed, miraculously survive the war – but not its aftermath.

By the fourth week of June 1918, *Jasta* 13 was entirely equipped with the D VII, and its scoring efficiency would steadily increase. This fine line-up shot shows ten Fokker-built D VIIs and one Albatros of the *Staffel*. All the machines display the blue fuselages and dark green noses of the *Jasta*. However, slight differences in pigmentation and perhaps the angle of sunlight produce markedly different tonalities for the blue fuselages on the orthochromatic film in use. First in line, marked with a white 'F', may be the aircraft of Uffz Johannes Fritzsche. Third in line is one of Heinrich Piel's Fokkers, marked with a white stork (apparently not 373/18 but a different aircraft). The Fokker fifth in line bears Albert Haussmann's engrailed band marking (*Dr V Koos via P M Grosz*)

TURNING POINT

The lack of suitable aircraft was further remedied on 28 June, when an allotment of 14 D VIIs arrived to be divided between *Jastas* 12 and 19. Even more welcome were six Fokkers powered by the superb 185 hp BMW IIIa engine, which went to Berthold's favourite *Jasta* 15. That evening, Büchner of *Jasta* 13 reached 'acedom' by downing a British scout. Niethammer recalled that Büchner had been a slow starter:

'When he was given the *Staffel* after Schwartz fell, he just managed to somehow "work down" his third and fourth with much trouble. But after this fifth victory he jumped out of his machine, came running to us over the field and shouted at once, "Now I've found it out men!" And he really had found it out, for since that day they fell left and right.'

On 29 June *Jasta* 13 was again in the thick of the action, as Büchner and Niethammer each claimed a SPAD but neither was credited. Uffz Fritzsche was luckier, destroying a Bréguet for his third confirmed opponent. However, the unit lost Uffz Heinrich Piel this same day when he was shot down behind French lines.

The *Geschwader* began gearing up for a move to a new airfield to participate in Ludendorff's final offensive toward Reims. The first day of

In terms of victories, Franz Büchner of *Jasta* 13 would survive the war as second only to Berthold in JG II with 40 confirmed claims. He had not emerged as a successful *Jagdflieger* right away, but his lengthy service and evident leadership skills earned him command of his unit in June 1918 when he had four victories. Seen here with an early Fokker-built D VII, he had hit his stride by July, and scored rapidly in August and September. His comrade Werner Niethammer wrote, 'In flying, Büchner was not that much superior to us. He was only that much better in the deciding moment, the moment when you smelled the castor oil and pushed the button. And that moment he had found out. He was probably the best shot I've ever seen, and had a brilliant eye' (*Helge K – Werner Dittmann*)

Jagdstaffel 13 pilot Uffz Heinrich Piel poses with his D VII 373/18, identified by his stork emblem and distinguished by the colourful bullet hole patches. The white serial number is visible through the blue paint. German records indicate that Piel was killed on 29 June, but an article in the French aeronautical journal *La Guerre Aérienne* stated this Fokker was shot down in flames on 30 June after the pilot had just shot down a French two-seater. The article reproduced this very photo, stating that it had been found on the burnt body of the pilot. Discrepancies like this are not uncommon in World War 1 aviation research

July brought a respite from combat for Berthold's weary *Staffel* 15 boys, as the *Kommandeur,* his technical officer Ltn Dingel and von Hantelmann left to attend the fighter type tests in Berlin, and the *Jasta* 15 pilots were 'put to rest' according to the war diary. This may well mean some of them were given leave, as *Jasta* 15 is conspicuously absent from the victory lists in July. *Jasta* 13, having received two more D VIIs on 1 July, was the only *Staffel* aloft that day, as Büchner and Niethammer both despatched Camels.

On the morning of the next day Büchner again led *Jasta* 13 over the front, and over Contay a single Sopwith Dolphin trailing streamers daringly attacked the Germans. Büchner engaged the RAF pilot, whom he recognised as a skilled and courageous flier. His opponent was Irish Maj J C Callaghan MC, the ebullient commander of No 87 Sqn, and a veteran with six victories, out on a risky lone patrol. The odds were stacked against the Irish ace, and Büchner shot him down in flames for his seventh victim.

Jasta 12 lost newcomer Vfw Hans Vietzen on 3 July – it was his first front flight, having arrived only the day before. The tireless Neckel claimed another Camel on the 3rd that would only be confirmed seven days later, by which time he had already downed another. Thus his 19th and 20th victories were confirmed out of order, but the 20-year-old from

The original caption for this fascinating photo states that Büchner is congratulating Ulrich Neckel on a victory. The specific occasion is unknown, but Neckel had obviously just returned from a flight and reported a success to his *Jasta* 13 CO, Franz Büchner. Neckel seems to have been flying his commander's D VII on this occasion, as the early Fokker-built machine displays part of Büchner's usual personal emblem of a green/white chequerboard band. Note the white 'Fok D' stencilling visible through the blue fuselage paint, and a cockade marking a bullet hole patch. Neckel was a proficient member of *Jasta* 13, attaining ten victories in June and July 1918
(*Helge K – Werner Dittmann*)

Mecklenberg was now in line for the *Pour le Mérite*.

As July wore on the JG II pilots faced new enemies in new ways. During the afternoon of the 4th, the *Geschwader* flew into the operational area of the 2. *Armee* to the north to strafe enemy troops. A foe of a different sort now being encountered was the 'Spanish flu'. The first signs of the influenza pandemic that would ravage Europe's population had now appeared, and on 6 July *Jagdstaffel* 19 could not fly because only three pilots were healthy.

Jasta 13 remained fit, though, and engaged No 209 Sqn again on the 7th. A patrol of Camels took off at 1000 hrs British time to intercept a German artillery spotter over Morcourt. Among the pilots were two Canadians that had participated in Richthofen's final combat of the previous 21 April – Wilfred 'Wop' May and Lt M S Taylor, a seven-victory flier, and the victor over *Jasta* 11 ace Hans Weiss. The Camels attacked the two-seater, but eight Fokkers led by Büchner came to the rescue. It seems that 'Sammy' Taylor fell to Büchner, spiralling in from 500 metres, while Neckel destroyed the Sopwith of Lt D Y Hunter.

Ltn d R Ulrich Neckel achieved his significant 20th success on 7 July 1918, thus putting him in line for the 'Blue Max'. Neckel duly poses with his green-nosed *Jasta* 13 Fokker to commemorate the occasion. He would go on to account for 30 enemies in all and receive the *Pour le Mérite* by the end of the war, although he was no longer with JG II by then

The next day, 21-year-old Vfw Richard Schneider of *Jasta* 19 scored his first of four victories when he despatched a fighter from SPA86. There was a personnel change on the 19th as the Adjutant Ltn *Freiherr* von Manteuffel was transferred to *Idflieg* (the Inspectorate of Aviation) and his duties were assigned to Ltn Walter Dingel, who retained his position as technical officer.

The *Geschwader* spent 12 to 14 July making the move to its new aerodrome at Leffincourt in the 3. *Armee*, giving the pilots a break from combat flying as Berthold (now back from Berlin) made plans for the offensive. The group had the honour of a visit from *Kogenluft* himself, *Generalleutnant* von Höppner, who expressed his gratitude for their sterling service. Berthold was given overall command of all the fighter units in the 3. *Armee* for the coming assault.

On 14 July the *Kofl* of the 3. *Armee*, Hptm Palmer, arrived to discuss the deployment of the *Jagdstaffeln* in the coming battle, and the popular Hermann Becker returned to finally take command of *Jasta* 12. That same day 20 new D VIIs were received – *Jasta* 12 got nine, *Jasta* 13 obtained three and eight went to *Jasta* 19. The war diary recorded, 'For the first time since its formation the *Geschwader* has been equipped with one type of aircraft, and looks forward with anticipation to the offensive which will begin on 15 July.'

FRIEDENSTURM

The Reims Offensive scheduled for the 15th would turn out to be Ludendorff's last great gamble. It was to be another strike in the Champagne, with assaults on both sides of Reims and plans to cross the Marne on a broad front – it was given the title of *Friedensturm* or 'Peace Assault'. The conflict that followed is often known as the Second Battle of the Marne or the Battle of Reims. The Germans had 48 divisions ranged against 43 Allied divisions, three of them American. Unfortunately for Ludendorff, his plans became as well known to the Allies as they were to his own men. As a result, the French were well prepared for the attack, and Foch was already planning his counter-offensive for the 18th.

The assault began with a four-hour bombardment, but this was preceded by a French counter-barrage of harassing fire. German assault troops then launched attacks to the west and east of Reims. The 3. *Armee* advance easily took the first French line, but this had been abandoned willingly. French artillery then pounded the German troops, and by noon the advance came to a standstill in this sector. The German armies to the west of Reims, however, succeeded in crossing the Marne and establishing a bridgehead. The JG II pilots were on alert from 0800 hrs onward, but Pippart of *Jasta* 19 claimed the day's sole victim, a SPAD south of Tahure.

On the 16th the JG II pilots were ordered to attack ground targets, but reportedly found nothing worth strafing. In the intense heat of the day the struggle for control of the air continued as Büchner accelerated his victory run with two Bréguets downed, taking his tally to ten. Meanwhile, Pippart and his *Staffel* mate Richard Schneider attacked SPA153, and soon two SPAD pilots were missing from the *Escadrille* roster.

Büchner's *Jasta* 13, however, had to mourn the death of 25-year-old Uffz Wilhelm Laabs, whose machine burst into flames at low altitude. This was probably another case of auto-ignition of phosphorus ammunition due to the high temperatures – a problem which plagued early D VIIs. Laabs reportedly jumped from his blazing aircraft at a height of only five metres and was fatally injured.

On the 17th the German advance west of Reims stagnated as Allied aircraft bombed and strafed the Marne bridges and tremendous air battles raged against the French in the 3. *Armee*. Pippart continued his deadly string, achieving his 18th victory by shooting a Bréguet out of a formation over the German lines and claiming another from the same group a few minutes later which remained unconfirmed.

Jasta 19 lost one of its most skilful pilots when Arthur Rahn was severely wounded in the hand and shinbone a day before his 21st birthday. He succeeded in landing at Leffincourt and was rushed to hospital, where he received the 'Hohenzollern' two weeks later. He recovered but never returned to combat flying, emigrating to the US in 1927.

THE TIDE TURNS

Marshal Foch began his counter-offensive on the 18th, launching American, Italian and French divisions – as well as 350 tanks – against the

German salient. On 19 July two *Jagdstaffeln* of the *Geschwader* were assigned to fly in the 7. *Armee* region to boost the strength of that army's fighter forces, and simultaneously JG II took over the aerial defence of the 1. *Armee*. The group encountered little enemy aerial activity over the 1. or 3. *Armee*, but there was plenty to make up for it in the hotly contested skies over 7. *Armee*. In all, the group made 95 front flights – 66 for the 7. *Armee* and 29 with 3. *Armee*. On this day the lethally consistent trio of Berthold, Büchner and Pippart each bagged SPADs, Berthold claiming a two-seater for his 38th.

JG II set a record of 100 front flights the next day, 20 July. Once again Berthold was victorious over a SPAD two-seater, but the resolute *Kommandeur* received serious hits in his engine, forcing him to land at Gemme in the 7. *Armee*. Newly-arrived Vfw Gustav Klaudat flew his own *Jasta* 15 Fokker to Berthold so that his leader could fly it back. Upon landing at Leffincourt, Berthold encountered a turbulent 'whirlwind' and wound up crashing Klaudat's D VII. The 'Berthold luck', legendary among JG II pilots, persisted, and he emerged unscathed, although a valuable Fokker was destroyed.

The next day no flights were made, as yet another move had been dictated by developments at the front. In the face of the Franco-American advances on the Marne, Ludendorff realised the situation was grave indeed. On the 22nd he decided to withdraw from the Marne. It was a turning point – from now on German forces, including JG II, would switch from offensive to defensive status.

Since Hans Pippart achieved both his 20th and 21st victories on 22 July, his commemorative wreath is marked with a '21'. This *Jasta* 19 OAW-built Fokker displays the unit's yellow nose and blue fuselage, but no individual marking can be seen. Pippart achieved only one more victory, and that was on the day of his death, 11 August 1918

Jagdgeschwader II airmen were now encountering the impressive, and formidable, Caudron R 11. The Caudrons were big twin-engined, three-seat escort fighters armed with five Lewis guns, and with nominal armour for the crew. They were meant to provide close-in fighter protection for the formations of Bréguet bombers when SPAD XIIIs were also available, the latter providing top cover for the Caudrons and bombers. The SPADs were free to pursue the attacking *Jasta* aircraft while the Caudrons stayed with the Bréguets – these tactics were a response to the heavy losses already suffered by the bombing *escadrilles*.

At 1030 hrs on 22 July, Pippart's *Jasta* 19 and other units tangled with just such a mixed formation – an estimated 30 Germans attacked 50 French aircraft. Pippart sent one of the big Caudrons down in flames, and topped this off with a SPAD five minutes later. Determined to obtain credit this time, he landed nearby to

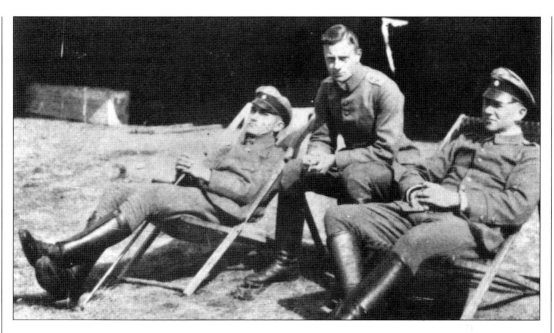

ensure the necessary confirmation for his all-important 20th and 21st claims – could the 'Blue Max' be far off?

Changes were in the wind. On 24 July the entire wing left the Champagne and moved north-west to Chéry-les-Pouilly airfield in the sector of the new 9. *Armee*. It may have been here that JG II received several SSW D IIIs and D IVs, the former having been modified to fulfil the specifications ordered after their first trial period. Also on the 24th, Ltn Dingel relinquished the duties of *Geschwader* Adjutant to the armoury officer Ltn von Buttlar, but Dingel remained technical officer for the group until replaced by Ltn d R Gerlt on 1 August.

On 28 July JG II received orders to deny the enemy any observation of the Aisne Valley, and to watch all traffic on eastern and northern roads. That day and the next saw victories for *Jasta* 13's Büchner and Ltn d R Grimm, and on the 31st Klein of *Jasta* 15 scored his 11th. 31 July also brought the posting of ex-observer Hptm Hugo Weingarth to the *Geschwader* staff.

The month of August opened impressively for Berthold as he reached the significant milestone of his 40th conquest, equal to the score of the legendary Oswald Boelcke. At this date only four other German aces had reached or surpassed it – the JG II leader received congratulations from General von Eben, commander in chief of the 9. *Armee*. Berthold identified his 40th opponent as an AR two-seater near Fére-en-Tardenois, but it was far more likely a Salmson 2A2 from the American 1st Aero Squadron, which lost two crews killed. The presence of Americans in the *Geschwader* victory log was a portent of many more to come.

BLACK DAYS

To the north-west, near the Somme, the crucial Battle of Amiens opened on 8 August. Ludendorff would call this 'the Black Day of the German Army', as the German lines were successfully shoved back as far as seven miles. The RAF made a gigantic contribution to this successful British

Jagdstaffel 13 pilots soak up the sun on the *Geschwader* airfield in the summer of 1918. They are from left, Ltn d R Kurt Hetze (five victories), Ltn d R Werner Niethammer (six) and Ltn d R Grimm (three). On 28 July Grimm downed his first victim (a SPAD fighter) over Chaudun

This happy pilot is the *Jasta* 15 ace Johannes Klein, although he is pictured here during his *Jasta* 18 era. Klein destroyed his 11th opponent on 31 July 1918, and followed that up with a Camel downed nine days later. He was credited with one of three SE 5s claimed by *Jasta* 15 on 11 August. Klein would end the war with the Knight's Cross with Swords of the Hohenzollern House Order, and either 16 or 18 victories (*Arthur Rahn collection, United States Air Force Museum*)

offensive. On 9 August JG II flew north to the 18. *Armee*, which was under heavy pressure. *Jasta* 15 seems to have tangled with Camels from 'A' Flight of No 65 Sqn at 1830 hrs, with von Beaulieu and Klein each claiming Sopwiths. Von Beaulieu also downed a SPAD for a double that day, and Berthold got a brace of French two-seaters to which Büchner added another.

The 10th dawned with the 2. *Armee* front under a mantle of thick fog, but the skies began to clear by noon for a day of maximum effor – and shocking loss – for JG II. At about 1220 hrs, a formation of 12 de Havillands from Nos 27 and 49 Sqns were bombing the railway stations at Péronne and Equancourt. They were attacked by JG II and other units, and one of the bombers fell to Berthold's close-range bursts. Almost immediately after this 'A' and 'B' Flights of the celebrated No 56 Sqn, joined by Bristols from No 48 Sqn, dived onto the Fokkers and a massive brawl followed as more SE 5s from No 32 Sqn waded in. In the confused melee fought under poor visibility, Veltjens, Borck, von Beaulieu and Berthold were all credited with SEs, while Büchner claimed a Bristol. No 32 Sqn lost one pilot killed and another as a PoW. No 56 Sqn's 'A' Flight leader, the respected five-victory ace William Boger, was killed over Marchelpot in the encounter with *Jasta* 15.

Berthold's D VII had been badly shot up, and suddenly the *Kommandeur* was shocked to find his control column broken off in his one good hand. His stricken Fokker was plunging earthward from only 800 metres. He briefly considered taking to his parachute, but in his semi-crippled condition he knew he could not manage the difficult gymnastics required by the release system. He grimly struggled to maintain control, but was unable to prevent his aircraft from crashing into a house in the village of Ablaincourt. The impact was so great the engine penetrated the roof to smash into the ground. German troops pulled the unconscious Hauptmann from the wreckage, amazed to find him still breathing. He had sustained further injury to his left arm, broken in the same spot as before. The *Kommandeur* was brought to Field Hospital 10 of the 2. *Armee*. The familiar 'Berthold-luck' (if one could call it that) held and he had survived another crash.

While the airmen of JG II were concerned about their leader's injuries, for some the news was perhaps a relief. His earlier good relations with many of his pilots had suffered. Paul Strähle and Georg von Hantelmann both recalled that, following his wound sustained in October 1917, Berthold – understandably – was only able to function and prevail against his horrific pain through the frequent use of morphine (Möller's history says only that he kept going with 'painkillers'). His usual highly critical behaviour had become increasingly erratic. In a typical instance, Berthold once criticised the condition of the group's quarters and airfield. 'The

Geschwader is a pigsty, a disorderly mess and this beastliness will end!', emphasizing his point by flailing away at his path with a riding crop. The demands on his nerves and pain-wracked body were simply too great. Now, however, the immediate concern was about his replacement. *Kofl* immediately decreed that temporary *Geschwader* command would be given to Hptm Weingarth, although Veltjens would lead in the air.

The eventful 10 August might have been even blacker for JG II, for Franz Büchner's career nearly ended as well. Niethammer described this day's work by *Jasta* 13:

'Right after take-off we ran into bad weather – low cloud and poor visibility. In the Laon sector we got into a dogfight in which Büchner shot down a two-seater and got himself put out of commission – that is, he received some hits in his fuel tank. The fuel leaked out and soaked him from top to bottom. He had the presence of mind to switch off the engine. Still, it was quite a piece of luck that he didn't get burned up. He landed somewhere in the terrain in the middle of the retreat operations and latched onto the last two machine gunners dropping back.

'Due to the bad weather, the dogfight and Büchner's forced landing, *Jasta* 13 really got scattered, which usually just didn't happen. I could only think of two or three times that we did not return to our aerodrome as a group, or at least in groups.'

Niethammer got lost in the fog, and almost landed in an Allied camp full of tanks. After getting 30 shots in his D VII, he beat a quick retreat and eventually landed at the airfield of JG I, to be told that three aircraft marked like his had landed at the nearby aerodrome of *Jagdgruppe* 10. There he re-joined Hetze, Grimm and an NCO pilot of *Jasta* 13. All four, as well as Büchner, made it back to Leffincourt by the evening. 'It was one of the wildest days I had ever experienced with *Jasta* 13.' In addition, *Jasta* 12 lost Ltn Muhs, who force-landed his D VII in French territory.

Although snapped during their *Jasta* 18 days, this photo of several of Berthold's *Jasta* 15 worthies might just as well have been taken in the successful summer of 1918. From left, they are Johannes Klein, Oliver von Beaulieu-Marconnay, Georg von Hantelmann (with cane), Hugo Schäfer and Hermann Margot. These young pilots formed a very close-knit band of *Jagdflieger*, and 'Beauli', von Hantelmann and Schäfer in particular were known as the 'Three Inseparables'. Of the group seen here, only von Beaulieu would not survive the war (*N W O'Connor*)

One eventful day followed another, and on a cloudy 11 August JG II achieved a record 12 victories, but suffered another crippling fatality. Veltjens pulled off the 'hat trick' in little more than a quarter of an hour to bring his own tally to 28. He started off at 1220 hrs by tackling a group of Caudron R 11s from *Escadrille* R239, and destroyed two of them in five minutes. Just ten minutes later he led *Jasta* 15 into a duel with 12 SE 5s from No 92 Sqn over Nesle, where the RAF machines were strafing the German aerodrome there. In this hard-fought scrap Veltjens, Klein and von Beaulieu were each credited with one SE 5. The RAF pilots lost Lt G Metson as a PoW, but in return they shot down the promising Gustav Borck of *Jasta* 15, who fell or leaped from his burning D VII.

At 1700 hrs the redoubtable Hans Pippart reverted to his old habits when he flamed a heavily defended British balloon at Brély. The 30-year-old from Mannheim was due for leave, and was engaged to be married, but this hardly dampened his eagerness to increase his score – the *Pour le Mérite* beckoned. At 1950 hrs, Pippart was back in the air at the head of his *Jasta* 19 to intercept a massive French bombing formation in the sector of Chauny–Noyon–Roye. There were over 100 Bréguets in groups of eight to ten each, once again escorted by the three-seater Caudrons.

The group came under heavy flak over Noyon, but Pippart still led his *Staffel* into combat against the trailing unit. Gefr Felder succeeded in sending a bomber of BR117 down in flames, but suddenly Pippart's D VII was seen to plunge earthwards near Guiscard. His pilots believed he had been hit by his own flak, while a R 11 crew from *Escadrille* C46 claimed to have downed one of the fighters. Pippart attempted to bail out at just 150 ft, but the parachute either failed or did not fully deploy and he was killed. His body was recovered and sent home to Mannheim. Coming so soon on the heels of Berthold's injury, this was another hard blow for JG II.

COMMAND DECISIONS

As a mere *Leutnant der Reserve*, the popular Veltjens was not qualified to take official full command of the *Geschwader*, and this was tacitly understood by

In July and August 1918, *Jasta* 12 was the least successful of the four *Staffeln*. It had fallen a long way from its glory days under von Tutschek, and even re-equipment with the Fokker D VII had little impact at first. On 10 August – the same day Berthold was wounded for the last time – the *Jasta* 12 pilot Ltn Muhs (who had only arrived two days earlier) became lost and force-landed his OAW-built Fokker behind the French lines. This overturned D VII under examination by French troops is thought to be the aircraft flown by Muhs, as it certainly seems to display *Jasta* 12 colours of a white nose, struts and blue fuselage. If there was a personal insignia on the fuselage, it would appear that some lucky *Poilu* has already cut it out for a souvenir (*J Guttman*)

the pilots. Nonetheless, there was considerable disappointment when *Rittmeister* Heinz *Freiherr* von Brederlow, leader of *Jagdgruppe* 11, was posted to acting command of the fabled *Geschwader* Berthold on 12 August.

Von Brederlow was an officer of long experience, but with only a single victory, he was hardly an inspirational figure. His time at JG II was brief. That very evening, the pilots were shocked when a car arrived at Leffincourt and out stepped a bandaged, but belligerent, Rudolf Berthold. The stern Hauptmann said simply, '*Hier bin ich der Herr!*' (Here, I am the master!) and von Brederlow amicably turned JG II back over to him. Berthold explained to his incredulous pilots that he had secretly escaped from the hospital to return, and managed to have himself transferred to the care of a doctor at *Kriegslazarett* 19E at Montcornet, where he wanted to recover and retain control of JG II. His first decision was to transfer Neckel from *Jasta* 13 to temporary command of *Jasta* 19 to replace Pippart.

On 12 August the *Geschwader* was held in reserve by order of *Kofl*, in anticipation of an attack against the 9. *Armee*. The unlucky 13th brought misfortune to another accomplished British ace at the hands of JG II.

Maj Charles D Booker, formerly a proficient exponent of the Sopwith Triplane, had 29 victories. He was now flying Camels as commander of No 201 Sqn, and on the 13th he was taking a new pilot on a tour of the lines. At 1200 hrs, west of Rosieres, the two were jumped by six Fokkers from *Jasta* 19 under Neckel. Booker put up a terrific fight, allowing his pilot to escape, but he eventually fell to Neckel's accurate fire. *Jasta* 19 lost a neophyte of its own this day when Ltn Schickler reportedly got lost over the lines. He may, however, have wandered into the fight and become Booker's final victim. Ironically, a year and two days before, on 11 August 1917, Booker had shot down and wounded *Jasta* 12 commander Adolf von Tutschek. Neckel had unknowingly avenged his former leader, bringing his own tally to 22 in the process.

All was far from well with the present JG II commander, however. Despite incredible pain and a high fever, Berthold stubbornly refused his doctor's urgent requests to return to the hospital. For all his faults, the ardent patriot Berthold valued duty above everything, and he believed his place was with his men as Germany faced its greatest threat. At this time a cable arrived with news of an imperial order sent via *Kogenluft* von Höppner:

'The *Kommandeur* of JG II, Hptm Berthold, must be given the order to place himself at once under treatment in a hospital and to stay there until his correct dismissal. Execution of this order, as well as the name and place of the hospital in question, must be telephoned to me via *Kofl* 9. Until further notice Ltn d R Veltjens will take over the command of the *Geschwader*.'

Berthold could hardly refuse a direct order from his supreme warlord

Although of poor quality, this photograph provides an important look at the famous red-nosed, blue Fokkers of *Jasta* 15 in the late summer of 1918. At extreme left is Gustav Klaudat's D VII, emblazoned with a black/white Uhlan lance and pennon, indicative of his former cavalry service. To the right of it is Joachim von Ziegesar's aircraft, marked with his usual insignia of three white feathers. Next is von Beaulieu's D VII, bearing his '4D.' emblem that was also a reference to his former cavalry regiment – it was based on the branding iron of the 4th Dragoons. The final aircraft displays an unidentified crowned shield in two colours. All of these D VIIs were Fokker-built machines, with wings in their factory 'lozenge fabric' finish

Hermann Becker finally took command of his cherished *Jasta* 12 on 14 July 1918, and under his guidance the unit slowly began to regain some of its former reputation as a crack outfit. On 11 August Becker began the resurgence of his *Staffel* by destroying a SPAD from SPA 37, and added an SE 5 from No 92 Sqn three days later. His tutelage would bear full fruit in September when *Jasta* 12 reached its zenith of performance. Becker would make it through the war with 23 confirmed victories, and narrowly miss the *Pour le Mérite*

Kaiser Wilhelm II, so he reluctantly assented and left the front for good. A letter written in mid-October reveals he still dreamed of returning to his *Jagdgeschwader*, but it was not to be.

With or without Berthold, the war went on. Veltjens assigned acting command of *Jasta* 15 to von Ziegesar. On 14 August seven British aircraft were shot down, with the honours shared between all four *Staffeln*. *Jasta* 12 was slowly improving under the guidance of Hermann Becker, who on this day led a flight of eight pilots, including Ltns Koch, Hans Besser, Herbert Bock, Alfred Greven, Vfw Wittchen and Flgr Rossbach. Besser wrote:

'Toward noon we flew to the front with eight machines to spoil the bombers' mission. Flak bursts at the far horizon drew us magnetically on. Between the Chemin des Dames and the Somme we saw a strong formation of enemy machines easily making its way. We flung ourselves roaring at them. Immediately, however, 15 single-seaters appeared out of the formation. At that moment a fierce aerial battle had begun, while the two-seaters continued on their way. A newcomer who flew with us lost his nerve – he immediately dived away.

'As soon as the fighters turned towards us, Bock and Koch also curved away toward the bombers to look for a victory there. Very soon they were miles off, and of no importance to the air fight any more. There were only five of us now against three times our number. Suddenly I saw two torches in the sky, but I could not say if we or the English had flamed an opponent. Everyone up in the air wanted to have a look at what was happening, and to join in the fight. Unfortunately, no German *Staffel* was near, only a 14-strong English formation, which immediately jumped on the pitiful little German band. From time to time you saw this marking or that flashing past, from which you could see that the five of us were still together.

'Suddenly I saw Greven crash-diving away sideways with two Englishmen behind him firing for all they were worth. To me it looked as if he was hopelessly lost. However, in the afternoon, he telephoned from Foreste where he had landed with a totally riddled engine. There were now only four of us against the English. And unfortunately we were only newcomers, or at least men of little front line experience – Rossbach, Wittchen and myself, who took up position with Becker.

'Our situation was extremely critical. I just turned in behind an Englishman and got him clearly in my sights. I had seen Becker to my right when I went for him and immediately my machine was hit. At the same moment I made a sharp turn. I saw two Englishmen diving at me, whose bursts were hitting me brilliantly. I heard the bullets go through the wings and into the steel-tubed fuselage. Becker had recognised my predicament at once and turned toward my antagonists. Both of us fired at them so that they let me go. A split second later I would certainly been lost. I was thankful to Becker for my life. The four of us now pulled into a tight formation to avoid giving the enemy a chance to attack. The English also turned off somewhat to reorganise themselves.

'We used this moment to abandon this fight, hopeless as it was for us. We dropped down for 2000 metres like stones and only then levelled off again. Our small *Kette* headed toward the airfield. In my mirror I could see the fuselage and tail of my machine. Everywhere shreds fluttered and a rudder cable was shot through, as well as the control column. I then

The first examples of the revolutionary Fokker E V parasol arrived at JG II in early August 1918. Among them was E V 128/18, seen with three happy pilots thought to be from *Jasta* 19. Note the streaky camouflage on both the aircraft wing and on the wings stacked in the background. The monoplane's sleek appearance promised great success, but disaster loomed for the new type (*P M Grosz*)

headed carefully toward Cherisy and made a very careful, soft landing – an "eggs" landing.'

Besser's Fokker was so riddled it had to be returned to the air park. The *Jasta* 12 pilots had survived an epic 20-minute battle, and Becker and Koch were both credited with victories.

Seven victories were notched up in the next two days. As the only *Staffel* equipped with BMW Fokkers, *Jasta* 15 was at the peak of its prowess. Gustav Klaudat chalked up the first of six with a SPAD on the 15th. Four more SPADs fell on the succeeding day, with claims by von Hantelmann, von Beaulieu and two by Veltjens. The lanky acting *Geschwaderführer* Veltjens had even more reason to celebrate that evening as the news of his overdue *Pour le Mérite* finally came. As was often the case, though, the day's elation was marred by a troubling loss.

JG II had received some examples of the revolutionary monoplane Fokker E V, powered by the Oberursel Ur II rotary engine. Ltn Ernst Riedel, a popular and promising pilot, met a tragic end in E V 107/18 on the 16th, as related by his friend Hans Besser:

'*Jasta* 19 had received the new Fokker single-seater for evaluation purposes. It was a monoplane with a 100 hp Gnome rotary engine and the wing above the fuselage, thus a parasol. Like all Fokker types without cables, the wing was made of plywood. Its improvements over the Fokker D VII were greater speed and manoeuvrability, and especially the excellent view afforded the pilot, particularly downward, since the lower wing was not in the way. Now Riedel flew the machine on display for us, most brilliantly.

'He was a wonderful pilot, almost too reckless. He flew all the figures, but unfortunately at too low an altitude. We could not hide our anxiety. Loops and turns do stress a machine, and too much is too much. Suddenly the wing came off. I could see how

Ltn d R Ernst Riedel of *Jasta* 19 is caught by the photographer as he poses on the wheel of his yellow-nosed D VII (OAW). This aircraft displayed Riedel's personal shield insignia on the blue fuselage, but precise details of this marking are lacking. Riedel had joined *Jasta* 19 from *Jastaschule* II in mid-May 1918. Although he scored no victories, he was recalled as being a 'brilliant pilot' by his contemporaries

On 16 August 1918, Ernst Riedel was putting on an aerobatics display for his fellow *Jasta* 19 pilots in one of the new Fokker E V parasols when the wing failed and parted from the fuselage. Riedel attempted to bail out, but the speed of the hurtling fuselage with the engine full on was too great and he was unable to exit the aircraft. With the death of a *Jasta* 6 pilot three days later, this led to the grounding of the new type and its eventual removal from the front (*Helge K – Werner Dittmann*)

Riedel tried to jump from the falling machine with his parachute. Already his upper body was out of the fuselage, but the speed of descent, with the engine at full power, was too great. The few hundred metres passed too soon. We did not watch the impact itself – we had already turned our heads away. But I can still hear the crash and then the complete silence. Only a few shreds of flesh and a pile of tubes were left.

'At the same time Koch (of *Jasta* 12) landed from a test flight with a Siemens Schuckert D III and crashed severely. He only came away with his life by a miracle.'

The loss of Riedel presaged the similar death of Ltn Rolff of *Jasta* 6 in a Fokker E V three days later, and these two accidents resulted in the grounding of the type and its removal from the front.

Jagdstaffeln 13 and 15 were clearly the ranking units of JG II during this period. From the start of *Friedensturm* through 17 August, Jasta 13 achieved 15 victories (mostly by Büchner) and *Jasta* 15 twice that number. Deadly air fighters though they were, the close-knit and longtime friends of *Jasta* 15 were still high-spirited young men.

On one sultry duty-free August day, they decided to pay a visit to the nearby airfield of the Richthofen *Geschwader*, which they had heard boasted a swimming pond. On the spur of the moment they decided to make their flight clad only in bathing gear, which surprised their hosts of JG I, who nonetheless quickly joined in for a refreshing dip.

Particularly popular, and mischievous, among the 'Berthold *Staffel*' was teenage Georg von Hantelmann. During the night shelling of Balatre back in April, von Hantelmann was cowering in a trench with the others when he suddenly jumped out and ran 'as if chased by Furies' back into his barracks. He quickly dashed back with a bottle of liqueur, saying he couldn't have lived with himself if it had been destroyed! On another occasion, wrote von Ziegesar:

'Hantelmann got into a silly mood. He apparently wanted to make a test flight, and when he was up he made one loop after another, perhaps

30 or more, like a crazy man. When we asked him what his point was, he said he had only wanted to find out if one would become dizzy! He loved to do crazy things. For a while it was a fashion in our *Staffel* to "sail" on the way back home, as we throttled down our engines and let our aircraft glide very slowly as far as possible. One day, as we were flying closely together, we did this again – and who can describe our astonishment as all at once the shrill trilling of a pea whistle sounded out in the air. It was Hantelmann, of course. Without saying a word to anyone, he had obtained the whistle from somewhere, and was now pleased as punch about his surprise. In

What the well-dressed (or undressed) German fighter pilot wore in the final summer of the war! In the steamy days of August 1918, one of the favourite pastimes of many JG II pilots consisted of a refreshing dip in the nearest pond or stream. This *Jasta* 13 group was photographed before Neckel left the unit on 12 August to command *Jasta* 19. From left to right, these out-of-uniform airmen are Grimm, Kurt Hetze, Ulrich Neckel, Franz Büchner (with a six-pointed star on his swimsuit), Werner Niethammer and an unknown pilot. Note that, with tongues firmly in cheek, some of these men even wear their badges and decorations. The pilots of *Jasta* 15 enjoyed a good swim as well, and once flew to the neighbouring swimming hole of the 'Richthofen Circus' clad only in their bathing suits

Franz Büchner's 19th and 20th victories on 20 August 1918 provided yet another opportunity for the customary JG II photo session. This early OAW-built Fokker D VII was decorated with the usual greenery and a special plaque which bore Büchner's chequerboard in the green and white Saxon colours along with his lion's head emblem

general, he could be so warmly happy that when his imminent laughter sounded out in our circle of comrades in the mess, he infected us all.'

On the 18th the staff and *Staffeln* 13 and 15 were relocated to the 18. *Armee* in the village of Foreste, north of Ham. They found that billets in the shell-torn village were already overcrowded by the army headquarters, and the airfield was modest at best. *Jagdstaffeln* 12 and 19 temporarily remained behind at Chéry-les-Pouilly.

The new airfield was dedicated by Büchner on the 9th when he shot down a Bristol near Pertain (this may have been one of two F2Bs from No 48 Sqn which collided during a dogfight). He continued his run the next day by destroying a SPAD from SPA155, and added a Bréguet to bring his score to 20 – he received his overdue 'Hohenzollern' that day, and no doubt looked forward to his 'Blue Max' before long.

While Haussmann of *Jasta* 13 also scored that day to reach half his commander's total, the *Staffel* lost one of its own when Offz-Stv Jakob Ledermann was shot down by SPADs. Ledermann was a promising Jewish pilot who had claimed his first victory over a Camel only six days before. He stated that he had shot down a French two-seater and then a SPAD before he himself was wounded in the leg and force-landed next to his erstwhile adversary to be taken PoW. Lengthy imprisonment and six operations would follow before he returned to Germany.

JG II continued its vendetta against French aircraft, making 53 front flights on 21 August and obtaining six victories. Ulrich Neckel brought the total victories of *Jasta* 19 to 60, and his own to 24, with a SPAD. Bréguet formations had been particularly aggressive in the afternoon, and *Staffeln* 13 and 15 attacked them determinedly, even though their own flak kept up heavy fire and endangered the German pilots. In addition, there were frequent conflicting victory claims made by flak and the JG II airmen, leading to strained relations between them. Nonetheless, the JG II war diary noted on the 23rd, 'In the period from 21 March to 21 August the *Geschwader* shot down 202 enemy aircraft, of which 83 fell to *Jasta* 15, 65 to *Jasta* 13, 30 to *Jasta* 19 and 24 to *Jasta* 12.'

A new airfield for *Jastas* 12 and 19 was found along the Fonfomme–Fontaine–Notre Dame road, and on 26 August the entire *Geschwader* transferred to it. The unit's personnel were just settling into comfortable quarters in the nearby village when frustrating orders were received shifting JG II to the 1. *Armee*. The group was to move to Neuflize aerodrome, but the mere seven lorries available prevented this from being

After the structural failure of his E V, Anthony Fokker arrived at the *Jasta* 19 airfield on 23 August to demonstrate his confidence in the strength of the E V's cantilever wing. With his usual flair for publicity, Fokker (in the white shirt with tie, walking toward the movie camera) convinced no less than 24 members of JG II to pose on the wing of an E V. Both still photos and motion pictures were made of this stunt, with *Jasta* 19 commander Ulrich Neckel featured prominently. Neckel is seated fifth from right on the wing in a light uniform, with his hand and cigarette to his mouth. When properly constructed, the cantilever wing of the E V was strong indeed. Nonetheless, the type was still grounded until a thorough investigation could be carried out. Inspections revealed that the interior wing surfaces had begun to rot from condensation moisture, and faulty assembly procedures and incorrect spar measurements were also to blame

Ltn d R Ulrich Neckel was unique among JG II aces, for he scored victories as a pilot in *Jagdstaffeln* 12, 13 and 19. Although a white-nosed *Jasta* 12 D VII (OAW) appears behind him here, it is thought this photo shows him as commander of *Jasta* 19 in August 1918. At the end of the month he left *Jasta* 19 for command of *Jasta* 6 in JG I, where he would finally receive his 'Blue Max' shortly before the war ended

Oblt Oskar *Freiherr* von Boenigk arrived on 31 August 1918 to take full command of *Jagdgeschwader* II. He was born on 25 August 1883 in Siegersdorf, in Silesia, and would become the final member of the triumvirate of JG II commanders. Although he did not as yet wear the 'Blue Max', he had attained 21 victories and would soon receive the Order. Von Boenigk would prove he was more than up to the task of leading the *Geschwader*

accomplished immediately. *Jastas* 12 and 15 made the move initially, while the other two *Staffeln* had to wait until the requisitioned vehicles were ready for their use.

The final day of August ushered in a vital development. Everyone had been wondering who the new permanent *Geschwader* leader would be. All speculation ended on the 31st with the appointment of Oblt Oskar *Freiherr* von Boenigk as the final commander of *Jagdgeschwader* II. This Silesian nobleman had just turned 25, and had been commissioned in the *Grenadier-Regt 'König Friedrich III' (2. Schlesisches)* Nr 11 in 1912.

He began his fighter career in *Jasta* 4 in JG I, then served successfully as commander of *Jasta* 21 for ten months. With his score at 21, he had recently been awarded the 'Hohenzollern', and would earn the *Pour le Mérite*. He soon proved to the JG II men that he was a worthy leader in the von Tutschek and Berthold mould. As was customary, he brought along a few personnel from his former *Jasta* 21 – Oblt Hans von Kalckreuth would serve as JG II intelligence officer and Vfw Karl Schmückle, along with von Boenigk himself, would now fly with *Jasta* 15.

The nomadic capabilities of a *Geschwader* were once again required on 2 September when orders came by phone to make the lengthy move to *Armee Abteilung* C (under Generalleutnant Fuchs) between the Meuse and Moselle rivers. The new airfields were located at Tichémont and Doncourt, near Conflans. At first von Boenigk was furious at yet another transfer, swearing into the telephone and roaring, 'With me you can do such a thing, eh?' to which the *Kogenluft* adjutant simply replied, 'You'll get plenty of work there.'

This time 25 lorries could be employed, and they embarked at noon on the 3rd. The staff and *Jastas* 15 and 19 flew to Tichémont, and *Jastas* 12 and 13 soon moved from Doncourt to Giraumont so that all four units were in close proximity. On this front the confident JG II veterans would encounter primarily American and, to a lesser extent, French opposition. A new commander, a new front and a new foe – although still on the defensive, JG II was entering a different and momentous era.

SPECTACULAR SEPTEMBER

As the pilots again settled into new quarters, they discovered that the high command of their new *Armee* was very pleased with their arrival. Formations of enemy bombers had been frequently raiding the vital railway centre of Conflans, or flying further on into Germany. Von Boenigk wrote:

'We learned that we faced Americans, and that our high command expected a large offensive in the coming days. The American pilots had complete air superiority and were numerically superior to our airmen. The single *Jagdstaffel* in our sector could not do anything against this superiority and therefore the upper command of the army had asked for a strengthening of fighter aircraft. On the day after our arrival, we could judge the impertinence of the American fliers when they quietly flew over Conflans at hardly 3000 metres altitude and dropped lots of bombs.

'Since our trains had not yet arrived, we could do nothing but look on in rage and promise revenge. In the afternoon the chief of staff of the army high command arrived to again inform me of the situation, and beg me to clean it up with all might as soon as we were ready.'

For the eager airmen of JG II, it was truly a target-rich environment. The *Geschwader* airfields were very close to the front, and von Boenigk had an observation post, constantly occupied, installed in one of the tall lime trees at Tichémont Park. The pilots also scanned the skies with binoculars and stayed on alert.

JG II lost one of its most valuable *Staffel* commanders and proficient air fighters at the beginning of September. Ulrich Neckel had been transferred to command of *Jasta* 6 in JG I. Therefore, Ltn Oliver Frhr von Beaulieu-Marconnay left his close circle of comrades at *Jasta* 15 to take over *Jasta* 19 on 4 September – ten days before his 20th birthday! The next few days saw little enemy aerial activity.

It was the lull before the storm. For some time the French and US commands had been planning an assault on the St Mihiel salient by the American First Army, scheduled for 12 September. It would be the first real test of an all-American army under American leadership. Col William Mitchell, commander of the First Army Air Service, had assembled a vast multinational air armada for this offensive. American and French squadrons made up the bulk of it, with elements of Britain's Independent Air Force (IAF). The total number of aircraft Mitchell had on paper was 1481, but in reality many of these were not fully serviceable. It is estimated that the Germans had approximately 213 aircraft in opposition, with JG II supplying a good part of the 70-plus fighters in place.

JG II opened its account on this front on 7 September when Vfw Haussmann and other *Jasta* 13 pilots attacked a Salmson 2A2 over Conflans at 1130 hrs, forcing it down in German territory. The crew of

With his BMW-engined D VII as a backdrop, the cheerful and garrulous Oliver *Freiherr* von Beaulieu-Marconnay is seen during his *Jasta* 15 service. Like Lothar von Richthofen, 'Beauli' had served in the *Dragoner-Regiment 'von Bredow' (1. Schlesisches)* Nr 4, and the branding iron emblem on his various aircraft was a reference to this. The D VII seen here may well have been one of Berthold's former aircraft, for his winged sword emblem appears to be seeping through the overpaint. The top wing uppersurface may be dark blue as well, with the off-white area on the starboard side possibly indicative of repair work. This aircraft was modified with a large windscreen and additional engine louvres. Von Beaulieu left *Jasta* 15 to take over *Jasta* 19 on 4 September 1918 (while still 19 years old), and contributed ten victories to the bag of JG II during the month

Lts A W Lawson and H Verwohlt of the US 91st Aero Squadron were taken prisoner. *Jasta* 19's new CO von Beaulieu claimed another Salmson for his 14th victory about an hour later.

ST MIHIEL

The storm broke in more ways than one on Thursday, 12 September. Low clouds, heavy rains and strong south-west winds lashed the entire front. At 0200 hrs the tempest was intensified by 2800 Allied guns opening up on the enemy lines. The Germans were only partially surprised, had expected an imminent attack and were already planning to evacuate the salient. Even before the infantry went over the top, American and French airmen had braved the thunderstorms and low ceiling to assist in the assault. In response, von Boenigk led the *Geschwader* into battle for the first time.

Berthold's harsh training and high standards would now pay great dividends as the crack pilots of JG II inflicted telling losses on the largely inexperienced Americans and their allies in the succeeding days.

Because the terrible weather that morning seemingly precluded flying, von Boenigk was trying to sleep in a bit longer, when:

'Suddenly I was awakened from my dozing by engine noise and machine gun fire. Fast as lightning I got out of bed and ran to the window. I did not trust my eyes – two American aircraft suddenly appeared out of the clouds and worked over our airfield with machine gun fire, without doing any damage. That was the limit! As suddenly as they had appeared they were gone. But they hadn't reckoned on us. Two pilots who had just test run the engines of their Fokker D VIIs jumped into their machines and off they went!

'A few minutes later the courageous Americans paid for their reckless action with their lives. Now, into our flying clothes and out to the machines! I announced an alert for the entire *Geschwader*. All morning long the "thick soup" stayed over our airfield and behind the front, so that the start of a *Staffel* or the *Geschwader* was impossible. Slowly the clouds disappeared and we could take off for our first formation flight at this front, which was to bring us further success. As always, I flew with *Jasta* 15.

'We had not been airborne long when we saw seven enemy aircraft about 100 metres above us and far behind. I immediately turned and recognised them as Americans of the Salmson type. They were returning from a mission. Because they were higher and faster, the attack was difficult. Nevertheless, two were downed, one (the only confirmed victim) by me. The victory was only possible by diving my Fokker in order to gain speed, then pulling up and firing upwards. The American wanted to escape, lost height, flew directly into my gun burst, lost a wing and spun down.'

Von Boenigk had started his JG II career by bringing down a Salmson of the 1st Aero Squadron in Allied territory. More sorties followed, and Büchner performed the 'hat trick', bringing his tally to 23 with three two-seaters. All were probably American DH 4s, with one likely from the 50th Aero Squadron – a group making its very first combat flights this day. *Jasta* 13's Hetze and Grimm each claimed American Bréguets to make it five for their *Staffel,* and Ltn d R Max Kliefoth of *Jasta* 19 cut his combat teeth with his first victory. The 19-year-old von Hantelmann scored a double with a Bréguet and a SPAD.

The pilot of the SPAD XIII was 1Lt David E Putnam DSC, a leading and popular ace of the US Air Service, and acting CO of the 139th Aero Sqn. Putnam – the same age as von Hantelmann – had flown with the French and had amassed 12 victories, with 15 or more 'probables'. *Jasta* 15 bounced the patrol he was leading at 1935 hrs and Putnam fell in American lines, shot twice through the heart. While JG II despatched nine enemy aircraft on the battle's first day, this had no affect on the progress of the American infantry that almost eliminated the salient by nightfall.

Friday 13 September would prove disastrously unlucky for both American fliers and a few of their JG II opponents. The weather was still rotten, with low cloud down to 100 metres, but once again aircrew from both sides set out into the murk. Von Boenigk solidified his leadership of the *Geschwader* with his second victim in two days. Gustav Klaudat, whose *Jasta* 15 D VII was marked with a black and white uhlan's lance, had an amazing day, doubling his score to six with three American SPADs.

Franz Büchner's brother Felix had arrived at *Jasta* 13 at the end of July, and on this day the two siblings accounted for three more SPADs, two of them falling to Felix for his initial victories. At 1535 hrs a flight of four Bréguet bombers of the US 96th Aero Squadron struggled off the muddy field at Amanty. After losing one aircraft to engine trouble, the remaining three bombed the ammunition dump at Chambley, but were immediately jumped by JG II Fokkers. Two of the bombers were shot down, apparently by von Beaulieu and Scheller. Their fellow *Jasta* 19 pilots Kliefoth and Ltn Gewert made successful claims, and von Beaulieu was later credited with a second Bréguet.

The day was not without loss for the *Geschwader*, however. Like many of his opponents, Ltn d R Eugen Kelber of *Jasta* 12 lacked experience, and had only made two combat flights since arriving 48 hours earlier. He became separated from his *Staffel* and was shot down in flames by two

FRANZ BÜCHNER

The youngest of three brothers to serve in World War 1, Franz Büchner was born on 2 January 1898 in Leipzig, the son of a wealthy business lawyer. He was still in school when the war came, but his brother Max was killed as a *hauptmann* on the Marne in September 1914.

To his parents' dismay, Franz enlisted in the 106th Saxon *Infanterie Regt* at the age of 16, and was in combat at Ypres by October. The next month he was seriously ill with typhoid fever, and could not return to his unit until February 1915. His performance so impressed his superiors that he was granted leave to complete his education, and was commissioned at the age of 17.

In 1916 Büchner was back with his unit at Verdun. On 3 April he was badly wounded in the lower abdomen, and would carry a piece of this shrapnel in his body from then on. After recovery, he was considered unfit for infantry duty, and thus joined the air service. He first flew with Fl. Abt. (A) 270, then joined *Jasta* 9 on 16 March 1917. Büchner broke into the scoring column with a Nieuport downed on 17 August, but this would not be confirmed for two months. By that time he had been transferred to *Jasta* 13 on 13 September, and had shot down a SPAD on 15 October. There followed a lengthy dry spell of eight months.

In June 1918, Büchner finally re-entered the victory lists with two SPADs credited on the 10th

and 11th. Four days later he was given command of *Staffel* 13 by Berthold, who evidently recognised the potential of the 20-year-old. His pace quickened in July, with seven aircraft destroyed. He improved upon this with eight more in August, reaching number 20 on the 20th of the month – the same day he received his 'Hohenzollern'. Büchner's torrid pace reached its zenith in September, when multiple victories on a single day became the norm. He was awarded the Saxon Knight's Cross of the Military St Henry Order on 7 October, and also the Mérite and Albert Orders in the grade of Knight 2nd Class with Swords. His final victory came on 22 October for a total of 40, and the long-delayed *Pour le Mérite* was announced three days later.

Having survived the war, Büchner was another of the ardent imperialists who joined the *Freikorps*. Having fought in upper Silesia, he was transferred to the *Fliegerabteilung Grossenhain*. On 18 March 1920 he flew a single-seater as escort for a reconnaissance machine assigned to locate Sparkist forces in his home town of Leipzig. Terrible weather forced the two-seater down, but Büchner stubbornly flew on to assist in the attack on the communist barricades and forces. During the return flight he crashed fatally near Mockau, probably due to ground fire. He had outlived his old commander Berthold by only three days.

Ltn Franz Büchner, commander of *Jasta* 13, was a veritable juggernaut in August and September 1918. Here, his ribbon bar displays his Saxon St Henry, Merit and Albert Orders ahead of the Prussian Iron Cross, 2nd Class, and the Hohenzollern House Order (*Courtesy L Bronnenkant*)

SPADs over Mars-la-Tour. In addition, Ltn Siebert of *Jasta* 15 was slightly injured in a crash landing at the airfield.

Yet it was not only the rookie pilots who made foolish decisions. Over eager to get confirmation for their six victories of the previous day, von Hantelmann and *Jasta* 13 pilots Hetze, Niethammer and the two Büchner brothers all piled into a car and headed for the front. Kurt Hetze jokingly remarked, 'Now I will drive to the front and get my wound badge.' They were unaware that the infantry's retreat from the salient was already in progress.

Ltn Werner Dittmann was the last *Offizier zur besonderen Verwendung* (*OzbV*), or adjutant, of *Jasta* 13. He had served as a pilot in Fl. Abt. (A) 222 in November 1916, and after attending fighter pilot school saw action with *Jasta* 1 on the Italian front in 1917. He was posted to *Jasta* 13 in May 1918, and was awarded the Iron Cross first class and the wound badge in black. He is seen here with two *Jasta* 13 OAW-built D VIIs behind him – the one in the hangar bears an unidentified personal insignia of a white diagonal sash (*courtesy Helge K – Werner Dittmann*)

This post-war portrait depicts the five-victory *Jasta* 13 ace Kurt Hetze, who narrowly escaped death during a strafing attack by a 95th Aero Squadron SPAD on Friday, 13 September. He seems to wear the wound badge in silver, awarded only for four or five wounds. He proudly displays his Saxon Knight's 2nd Class with swords badge of the Mérite and Albert Orders, his Iron Crosses of both classes and his pilot's badge

From nowhere a low-flying SPAD swooped out of the clouds and made a strafing run on their vehicle. The car screeched to a stop and all five pilots unglamorously flung themselves into a ditch as the fighter's bursts kicked up gravel around their heads. During the second pass, Hetze suddenly spouted blood from his nose and mouth as he took a bullet in the lungs. After three more passes, the American finally left and the others helped Hetze into the car. They were racing back to their aerodrome when two more SPADs appeared with similar intentions. Once again the car was stopped and the five managed to find cover behind a house, walking around it to keep the building between them and the aircraft. Hetze later wrote:

'On this occasion we met a Hungarian officer of high rank who bade me drink from a small bottle of French cognac, which did wonders for my situation. He wanted to propose Franz Büchner and myself for a Hungarian decoration. Then Felix Büchner brought me to *Feldlazarett* B37 at Valloy.'

Hetze's war was finished. The SPAD pilot who had narrowly missed ending the careers of four other prominent airmen was almost certainly 1Lt Sumner Sewall of the 95th Aero Squadron, who had already claimed four of his eventual seven victories. On 13 September he reported he had strafed a staff car with five officers in it, who jumped out into a ditch – the descriptions from opposite sides parallel each other very well indeed.

The 13th also brought bad and good fortune to Rudolf Rienau of *Jasta* 19, who recounted:

'At 1930 hrs I took off for the lines with a flight of four Fokkers and attacked six SPADs at 3000 metres. While I was pursuing one, another caught me from behind and shot up the control cables and apparently the rudder. The aeroplane plunged downward and could not be controlled no matter what I tried. At about 500 metres I tried for one last time and pulled

the machine up, but then my seat broke and the aircraft nosed into a left-hand bank. Thereupon I unbuckled the safety belt, let myself flop out backwards to the left, banged my shoulder on the tail and after a very short fall, floated down. I spun around in my parachute several times, then hung very quietly, got my orientation and spied German soldiers on the ground.

'Hitting the ground north of Charey, I tried to land upright but fell half on my side and half on my back. Because of the low altitude I couldn't pull the brake shroud line, and therefore hit quite hard, but without injury. My aircraft lay about 150 metres from me, completely destroyed.'

The third day at St Mihiel – 14 September – brought better weather, with a high ceiling and good visibility providing the perfect setting for a day of unparalleled effort and success by JG II. On the other side of the lines, the American First Day Bombardment Group prepared for its first day of full group operations. Formed four days before, it consisted of the experienced 96th Aero Squadron flying Bréguets and the newly formed 11th and 20th Aero Squadrons, both flying DH 4s with Liberty engines.

An unidentified JG II pilot agreeably demonstrates how the canopy of the new parachute would deploy on a breezy summer's day in 1918. To the left behind the billowing 'chute is the tail of a captured SPAD, suitably marked with German insignia, and to the right is a green-nosed Fokker of *Jasta* 13. The parachutes and the Heinecke harnesses were still relatively new devices, and there was considerable scepticism about them. Even though several notable pilots were killed when their parachutes or harnesses failed for various reasons, trust in the devices slowly grew. Rudolf Rienau of *Jasta* 19 apparently made the first successful descent of a JG II airman on 13 September 1918 when he was shot up by a SPAD (*courtesy Helge K – Werner Dittmann*)

The Bréguet 14 bombers of the American 96th Aero Squadron formed part of the beleaguered First Day Bombardment Group, and were frequent opponents (and victims) of JG II. The airmen pictured with this Bréguet 14A2 were, however, two that 'got away'. The pilot, Lt Bradley Gaylord, and his gunner, Lt Howard Rath, led three aircraft of 'A' Flight on a raid against Chambley on 13 September. The other two bombers in the flight were shot down by *Jasta* 19, and only this crew returned to tell the tale

All three squadrons were ordered to attack Conflans. It was the first time American-built DH 4s made a bombing raid over the lines. A formation of seven DH 4s of the 11th Aero Squadron succeeded in bombing the railway yards, but as soon as they turned for home a group of expertly flown red-nosed Fokkers from *Jasta* 15 dived into their defensive V formation. One of the Americans recalled that each D VII, 'attacked with a quick climbing turn, a short burst of fire, a stalling turn, a sharp side-slip toward the other side of the "V", and a repeat of the same manoeuvres. Thus one fighter could attack both sides in a single pass.'

All of the American bombers were badly riddled, and two were sent crashing to earth at 0900 hrs by von Hantelmann and Weischer.

Ulrich Neckel caught an artillery-spotting Bréguet 14A2 from BR243 and shot it down near Metz.

Later in the morning *Jasta* 15 was airborne again, and it made a classic out-of-the-sun pounce on eight SPADs from the 22nd Aero Squadron. 1Lt Arthur Kimber was flying 'tail-end charlie', and wrote home:

'So when the nine Fokkers attacked us, Little and I were the first victims. About four of the red-nosed, blue-bodied machines jumped on me. They had height and were in the sun, and all I could do was wriggle. At that moment I looked below and saw that five or six other Fokkers had come up and were attacking the rest of the patrol. In a dogfight like that, it soon develops into each man for himself, and the devil take the hindmost. Well, I was the hindmost!

'One especially attracted my attention, and he was only about 75 metres off. He moved prettily, and I moved like mad to get out of his sights. With motor racing at full speed, I swung into a fast, steep right-hand spiral dive, going down almost vertically, and yet turning enough to keep the other fellow's sights off me. Then the Boche seemed to pull out of the following dive, evidently convinced that he had sent a SPAD down out of control. There were nearly 70 holes in my machine, mostly in the fuselage and body. The rudder control wires were nearly cut in two.'

Along with Kimber and 2Lt Little, 1Lt A 'Ray' Brooks also narrowly survived this harrowing encounter with the 'red-nosed nightmares' and returned with a shot-up aeroplane. He was credited with two of his six victories this day, and never tired of telling the story the rest of his long and ebullient life. However, the Americans did lose 1Lt P Hassinger, whose aircraft exploded when the fuel tank was hit. By the end of the day, von Boenigk, Klein and von Hantelmann had notched up two SPADs apiece, with Schmückle getting another to take *Jasta* 15 past the milestone of 150 victories.

Every *Jasta* in the group had multiple victories on the 14th, with *Jasta* 19 claiming four American two-seaters. The day's sacrifice was not limited to Yanks, however, as *Escadrille* BR132 provided the targets for *Jasta* 13. Büchner and his

Siemens-Schuckert Werke D IV 7553/17 was first despatched to JG II in April for frontline testing. Like the other Siemens fighters, it suffered engine problems and was sent back to the factory for modifications and a new engine. It was returned to *Jasta* 12 in July, and is seen here with a cut-away cowling and a smaller spinner fitted with ventilation louvres. The interplane struts appear to be white, while the wheel covers were five-colour fabric (*A Imrie*)

Staffel virtually annihilated a flight of Bréguets. Five of the bombers failed to return from their mission, with Büchner destroying three and Niethammer and Grimm the others. 14 September witnessed a record 19 confirmed claims by JG II for the loss of one pilot made PoW. This accomplishment would remain unsurpassed in the *Geschwader*'s history. At the end of the day the entire group gathered for a raucous victory feast. Ltn Dingel proposed a toast to von Boenigk, duly recognising him as a worthy commander, and no doubt kicking off a very wet evening.

The success of the German fighter pilots was not matched by their infantry compatriots, who were pulling out of the salient on 15 September. Allied bomber squadrons persisted in their valiant attempts on that Sunday, and (despite their partying of the previous night) JG II pilots made 69 sorties. The consistent Büchner claimed two SPADs, his fourth 'multiple' in as many days (nine victories since 12 September).

Von Beaulieu celebrated his 20th birthday with a SPAD, one of three scalps for *Jasta* 19. The day's most notable action, however, was the decimation of No 104 Sqn of the IAF. Two flights of DH 9s from the unit followed No 99 Sqn to successfully bomb the railways near Metz Sablon, but the second formation fell behind on the return trip, and the shadowing D VIIs in the sun took the opportunity presented them. Once again they were the 'red-noses' of *Jasta* 15, who were by now experts at breaking up bomber formations.

Jagdgeschwader II had record success on 14 September, achieving 19 victories shared between all four *Staffeln*. The only casualty suffered was the loss of Ltn d R Paul Wolff of *Jasta* 13, who was taken prisoner when he was shot down over Lake Lachaussée at 1510 hrs. His OAW-built Fokker D VII fell into American hands entirely intact, and became the subject of numerous photos. This view shows off Wolff's personal emblem of a white arrow on the blue fuselage, and the 'new' version of the *Jasta* 13 green nose marking, limited to the forward engine cowling and bordered by a white band. This green and white nose was instituted at the behest of the CO Franz Büchner, perhaps in reference to his Saxon origins. The upper cowling of Wolff's D VII seems to be a lighter shade than the green side panels, and may have been a replaced component. The wheel covers were dark green like the nose, and the wings retained their four-colour fabric finish. This photo shows an American DH 4 and SPAD in the background

The captured *Jasta* 13 Fokker of Ltn Paul Wolff eventually turned up at Colombey les Belles in the company of a 'white' SE 5 and various Nieuports and a SPAD. Other views show several bullet hole patches on the port side of the cockpit area and lower wing, indicating that 14 September was not the first time it had seen combat. Wolff was a relatively new pilot, and had no victories when he was shot down

The Fokker pilots dived on the de Havillands and closed in to very close range. Schäfer, Weischer and von Hantelmann each gained credit for one DH 9 downed, but the *Jasta* 15 pilots had seriously under-claimed for once. Of the 12 crews of No 104 Sqn that set out, only five landed back at their field at Azelot. One two-man crew was killed out-right, two more were made PoW (one of the pilots later died of his wounds), two aircraft crash-landed in Allied lines with wounded or injured crews and another pilot brought back a dead observer.

By 16 September the American frontline was firmly established from Vandieres to Haudimont, and the St Mihiel drive was finished. American infantry units were already being pulled out to take up new positions for the Meuse-Argonne campaign, but aerial combat continued over the St Mihiel sector.

French and American SPAD pilots had waged an aggressive campaign against German balloons during the offensive, succeeding in obstructing the enemy's view of the battlefront. The famous Frank Luke Jr and Joseph Wehner of the US 27th Aero Squadron had claimed nine balloons in the five days since the drive began. The French pilots of SPA77 had also pursued a rampage against the 'gasbags', led by their top scorer Sous-Lt Maurice Boyau. On 14 September Boyau and two others destroyed one of the tethered targets, and together with a trio of other SPA77 airmen had burned two more on the 15th, bringing Boyau's personal tally to 20 balloons and 14 aircraft.

On 16 September Boyau again teamed up with Cpl Walk, Aspirant Cessieux and American Cpl Corsi of his unit, and had flamed another balloon at 1120 hrs when *Jasta* 15 intervened. The French ace dived

A few of the reconditioned SSW D IIIs also went to *Jasta* 15, as evidenced by this red-nosed machine displaying a white 'V' of unknown significance. The spinner was not painted red at the time of this photo, but remained bright metal (*A Imrie*)

A different perspective of the *Jasta* 15 SSW D III reveals the wing crosses painted at extreme outboard locations. Unfortunately the pilot of this *Jagdstaffel* 15 aircraft remains an enigma (*A Imrie*)

beneath the flaming balloon to try to drive away the Fokker chasing Walk. However, Boyau's machine was hit either by ground fire or by rounds from one of the D VIIs and fell in flames. The three remaining SPAD pilots were all wounded, but returned safely. Von Hantelmann apparently received credit for Boyau's SPAD and Klaudat was allowed another.

On the same day *Jasta* 19 savaged a flight of four Bréguets from the 96th Aero Squadron, sending three down in flames and bringing the crew of the fourth down as prisoners, although only three aircraft were credited.

Franz Büchner's heated pace continued on the 17th with another double to bring his score to 30 – he was scoring so rapidly the Orders Chancellery could not keep up with him, and his *Pour le Mérite* was overdue. Meanwhile, the 95th Aero Squadron lost another pilot to JG II when von Hantelmann shot up the SPAD of Lt Waldo Heinrichs, who would survive his terrible wounds and ordeal in German PoW camps.

On 18 September the 27th Aero Squadron team of Luke and Wehner was back at work, burning two more captive balloons near Labeuville. Once again, *Jasta* 15 arrived too late to save their balloons, but took revenge on the victors. Wehner was mortally wounded by the proficient von Hantelmann and came down behind German lines – he died a few hours later in a field hospital.

Meanwhile, multiple victories had become routine for Franz Büchner, the bane of American SPADs – he destroyed two more this day. One of his

Only four weeks after his 20th claim, Franz Büchner was again posing for the photographer, this time in celebration of his 30th victory on 17 September. Büchner, seen with his usual lion's head plaque and floral wreath, was particularly successful against American SPAD fighters. He scored the lion's share of *Jasta* 13's September victories, with 17 of the unit's 27 opponents falling to his guns opponents put up a splendid fight and flew with great skill, but was still defeated – this was probably 1Lt David McClure of the 213th Aero Squadron, who became a PoW.

THE BEWILDERMENT GROUP

Many of the impressive successes of JG II in September came at the expense of the American First Day Bombardment Group. As noted, the group had been hurriedly assembled on the eve of St Mihiel by throwing together the novice 11th and 20th Aero Squadrons (DH 4s) with the 96th Aero Squadron (Bréguets), the latter outfit having seen service since mid-June in the quiet Toul sector. Few of the crews of the 11th or 20th had any frontline experience, and were rushed into combat without time to practice flying bomb-laden DH 4s. The group suffered from inept leadership and poor tactics, and after severe losses, the remaining crews began to sarcastically refer to themselves as 'The Bewilderment Group'.

The nose-heavy DH 4s, powered by the untried Liberty engine, gained a reputation as 'flaming coffins' – the group did in fact lose seven of these machines in flames. Even the relatively seasoned Bréguet crews of the 96th were hampered by faulty command decisions. They were forced to learn from bitter experience that small formations of less than squadron strength, sent in succession over the same target, had little chance against determined German fighter units of the calibre of JG II. Yet the courageous bomber crews persisted in their missions, and not one of the group's formations was ever turned back by enemy attack

Sadly typical was the mission flown by the 96th on 16 September. Eight Bréguets took off from Amanty at about 1700 hrs to bomb Conflans, but four crews dropped out due to engine problems before crossing the lines. The remaining four unwisely pressed on and successfully bombed the target, but soon came under attack by *Jasta* 19 and other elements of JG II (one crew reported 24 enemy aircraft). The crew of 1Lt Charles Codman and 2Lt Stewart McDowell put up a stubborn defence, but could only watch grimly as each of the other three bombers were sent down flaming in their turn. Then McDowell was badly hit in both thighs and Codman was slightly wounded in the leg.

Fortunately they were flying a new Bréguet 14A2 with a disposable fuel tank, which Codman jettisoned. They spiralled down to a crash landing and were taken prisoner. Codman survived to become Gen Patton's aide in World War 2. Although the entire flight of four aircraft was destroyed, *Jasta* 19 was credited with only three confirmed claims, those going to von Beaulieu, Felder and Rienau.

Two days later the opportunity came knocking for *Jasta* 12. This unit had been the least successful of the four *Staffeln* in recent weeks, with only a single victory in the past month. Its luck changed at 1730 hrs on the 18th when a formation of six DH 4s from the 11th Aero Squadron arrived over Conflans. Becker was leading seven Fokkers in 'V' formation home from a patrol when they spotted the bombers. The *Staffelführer* fired a red flare and his men fanned out into a line abreast and closed with the Americans. Hans Besser told the tale:

'The earth was almost completely covered by balls of clouds, and the holes in between were very hazy. We were high above it at 4000 metres, and searched the sky for enemies. It looked to us as if the weather had been

Ltn Herbert Bock was a *Jasta* 12 veteran, having been posted to the unit in January 1918. He flew this OAW-built D VII in the late summer of 1918, and his personal marking was another visual pun signifying his surname. 'Bock' literally means 'ram', thus his choice of insignia. The ram's head was apparently placed over a previous banded marking which has been painted over. Note the tubular gunsight and the light rib tapes on the four-colour fabric on the wing (*courtesy A Imrie*)

made for bombing attacks, for it allowed a covered approach between the clouds. And surely, we had not been mistaken. They flew cleverly around every mountain of cloud and stayed in the valleys, thereby using the light and shadow as camouflage. The colourful cockades, however, betrayed them to us, and we dove vertically down into them. What followed happened within a matter of seconds.

'We fell onto the formation like a hailstorm, and the observers hardly had time to fire at us. We used the Fokkers' speed to hang immediately at their tails. Almost all of us had an opponent in front of us. Becker and myself fired almost simultaneously at two Americans. Mine waited to take fire while Becker was so fast he had already produced the first torch in the sky. Almost at the same moment Becker's second victim also caught fire, as did my American. And of the other enemies, there was nothing to be seen any more – only some thick pillars of smoke stood over the clouds.

'We flew through the cloud bank and only then saw that we were close to Conflans. Below us there were the burning machines, almost in a row, and some kilometres to the front the other two. Our airfield was only three kilometres off, and we landed at once. The joy of my mechanics also knew no bounds, for they felt of themselves as sort of fliers too.

'Before it got dark, we drove over to Conflans to look over the wreckage of the fallen foe. We had won out against the latest American aeroplanes. They were DH 4s, with 400 hp engines of the latest design. The equipment and gear were splendid. However, the Fokker D VII had shown itself superior to the enemy's latest advances in speed.'

At Giraumont, the *Jasta* mechanics had seen blazing aircraft fall out of the cloud layer like torches in the waning light, but had been unable to determine their identity. Their concern turned to jubilation when all seven Fokkers buzzed the airfield before landing. The victories were parceled out in this way – Hermann Becker got two and Greven, Besser,

Ltn d R Hans Besser of *Jasta* 12, who participated in his unit's successful decimation of American bomber formations on 18 and 26 September, flew this D VII (OAW) in the summer of 1918. The Fokker bears the usual dark blue and white colours, with Besser's personal broom insignia in white. This was another play on words related to the pilot's surname, as the German '*Besen*' translates as broom. Besser achieved his only two confirmed victories during the attacks on the DH 4 formations from the 11th and 20th Aero Squadrons (*A Imrie*)

and Flg Wilke each received one. The sixth DH 4, flown by 1Lt V P Oatis and 2Lt R Guthrie, only just managed to escape by skilful dodging through the clouds to return so the crew could tell their sad story.

The accomplishments of the *Geschwader* were recognised in the army communique of 20 September:

'Over the battlefields between the Meuse and Moselle, *Jagdgeschwader* II, under the command of Oblt *Freiherr* von Boenigk, shot down 81 enemy aircraft between 12 and 18 September, losing only two of their own in battle.'

The infantry and artillery in the sector were also deeply grateful for the efforts of JG II. Von Boenigk received some unusual rewards as a result of his command's success:

'The enthusiasm of some officers was equally great, and the *Kommandant* of the staff quarters of the army, a reserve major and famous dental professor in civilian life, put my teeth in order for nothing!

'On 20 September I was about to take off when a soldier came running up to my machine and told me that the commander-in-chief had arrived and wanted to talk to me. I climbed out of my Fokker and reported myself in full flying dress to his excellency Generalleutnant Fuchs. He said something to me like, "I have personally come to you as commander of the victorious *Geschwader* in order to thank you and your brave pilots personally, and, in the name of the army, to express my special thanks for the excellent achievements of the last few days." Thereupon he shook my hand, had some aerial combat experiences related to him, and asked me if

This splendid view of *Jasta* 12 is thought to show Giraumont airfield in September 1918. Visible are two OAW-built Fokkers, one SSW D IV and five SSW D IIIs of *Jasta* 12. The Siemens fighters had been modified to meet *Idflieg* specifications following their first brief service period, and had been arriving at JG II since July. The third Siemens from the left displays the white lightning flash of Ltn d R Alfred Greven. The second Fokker from the left and the SSW D IV 7553/17 adjacent to it both bear a single white band as a personal marking, and were probably flown by the same pilot. The Fokker pilots of *Jasta* 12 downed 11 opponents in September (*A Imrie*)

I had some wishes for the *Geschwader* as to provisions, etc. My wishes regarding wine, tobacco, chocolate, etc. were met completely, and the next day several lorries arrived with wonderful contents, which were greatly appreciated by all.'

There may have been ample wine and chocolate, but on 22 September the war diary noted the scarcity of more vital supplies:

'The shortage of fuel which arose some time ago can lead to the most serious problems during the large battle activities which must be reckoned with. Aerial superiority will hang in the balance. The *Staffeln* have been put on rations of 450 litres per day, which will be only one-fifth of the real need. For four take-offs with eight aeroplanes, each *Staffel* uses 3500 litres. Requests to the *Kofl* had no result.'

The 23rd brought another eminent guest when *Kogenluft* von Höppner visited JG II to express the Kaiser's and his own gratitude for their deeds. Unfortunately this appreciation did not extend to any medals or extra fuel rations. In the morning of that day von Beaulieu of *Jasta* 19 achieved his momentous 20th victory and von Hantelmann accounted for a DH 4. During the evening the *Geschwader* entertained Oblt Hermann Göring

Another view of the same mixed line-up of Fokker and Siemens fighters of *Jasta* 12 shows up the dark blue and white unit markings of these beautiful machines. The fin and rudders of all the aircraft were painted white

This rare photo commemorates von Bealieu-Marconnay's 20th victory, achieved on 23 September when he was credited with a Bréguet 14 (actually probably a Salmson 2A2 from SAL28). 'Beauli' is seen with his appropriately decorated D VII on the field at Tichémont, along with his pilots from *Jasta* 19. From left to right, they are Ltn Scheller (four victories), Ltn Fritz Gewert (two), Ltn d R Wilhelm Leusch (five), von Beaulieu, Ltn Rudolf Rienau (six), Ltn d R Max Kliefoth (three) and Ltn Hans Körner (six) (*courtesy A Imrie*)

and others of JG I. The Richthofen *Geschwader* had just moved to Metz-Frescaty airfield, but the two groups encountered little enemy aerial activity in the following two days, as the Americans shifted forces for their final great battle of the war.

THE MEUSE-ARGONNE OFFENSIVE

At 0330 hrs on 26 September a cacophonous three-hour barrage kicked off the Meuse-Argonne assault by the American First Army. It was launched along a 20-mile front, from the River Meuse in the east to the rugged heights of the thick Argonne Forest to the west. Three extremely strong lines of defence were manned by the German 3. *Armee* and the 5. *Armee* to the north-west. Allied aerial forces available for this assault numbered about 800 aircraft, three-quarters of them American.

In response to this news, JG II flew into the sectors of the two armies under attack. At 0800 hrs the First Day Bombardment Group launched three squadrons to bomb Dun-sur-Meuse. Once again they followed the reckless tactic of sending three small formations to the same target in close succession. The third group consisted of seven DH 4s from the 20th Aero Squadron that were attacked at soon as they crossed the lines.

For the second time in nine days, *Jasta* 12 decimated a formation of DH 4s. After bombing the objective the lead DH 4, flown by 1Lt Howard, was hit and the dead observer fell into the cockpit, jamming the control cables. The pilot could not regain control and unwillingly flew east deeper into enemy territory, followed by his squadron, directly into the path of Becker and *Jagdstaffel* 12. Becker destroyed two of the bombers in short order to bring his tally to 18, and Besser gained his second victory with another. He had watched transfixed as the observer climbed onto the fuselage of his flaming machine and jumped headlong into space – a moment later the bombs on board the DH 4 exploded.

Before his guns jammed, Ltn d R Alfred Greven shot up the aircraft of 2Lt G Wiser and 1Lt Richardson badly enough to force it down. Wiser glided his powerless, riddled DH 4 down to a safe landing right on the *Jasta* 12 field at Giraumont, where the American crew was entertained by the *Staffel* before being shipped off to a prison camp.

Vfw Otto Klaiber fastened on to the DH 4 flown by 1Lt Merian C Cooper, who later recalled:

26 September was yet another red-letter day for JG II, with *Jasta* 12 annihilating a flight of DH 4s from the 20th Aero Squadron. Two lucky survivors were Lts Glenn Richardson (pilot) and Guy Brown Wiser, who were forced down by Alfred Greven as his second victim. Even with a dead engine and landing downwind, Richardson managed to side-slip the DH 4 down to a fine landing right on the *Jasta* 12 field at Giraumont, where the two-seater is seen surrounded by groundcrew. Richardson had a slight flesh wound in his right leg, and Wiser had a wounded foot. Richardson later wrote, 'A German pilot obtained first aid bandages for both Wiser and myself, and shortly after we were given a meal at their mess hall. The German pilots did no questioning whatever, and seemed inclined to be very courteous and pleasant, for on leaving, they filled our pockets with cigarettes and managed to return the clothes taken away on landing.' Richardson also recalled how Greven sat across from them in the mess hall and gleefully added his latest victory to the *Jasta* chalkboard record (*A Imrie*)

A view of the pristine DH 4 No 32286, flown by Richardson and Wiser of the 20th Aero Squadron on the *Jasta* 12 field at Giraumont on 26 September 1918. The DH 4 was obviously a prize trophy, and the second of Alfred Greven's four confirmed claims (*A Imrie*)

This fine shot provides details of classic *Jasta* 12 markings as applied to an OAW-built D VII. The two vertical white bands were the pilot's personal insignia. Note the pale rib tapes that are quite prominent against the four-colour printed wing fabric. A rear-view mirror is fitted and a rack for flare cartridges is mounted on the side of the cockpit. Once again, a Morell airspeed indicator is affixed to the port interplane strut (*A Imrie*)

'My observer, 1Lt Edmond C Leonard, was shot through the neck. The shot came out through his shoulder and knocked him into his cockpit. I received a graze across the head which stunned me. Although severely wounded and bleeding heavily, my observer endeavoured to carry on the fight, but collapsed. As my engine was hit, and I was unable to keep up with the formation, I was quickly surrounded by enemy aeroplanes.

'Just at the instant of kicking into a spin in order to make myself as poor a target as possible, my engine caught on fire. I fell one or two turns into a spin, during which time my hands and face were burned. By putting the aeroplane into a nose-dive and opening the throttle wide, I was able to burn out the gas in the engine and extinguish the fire.

'I crashed the aeroplane on landing, snapping the landing gear and breaking the propeller. My observer and I got out of the aeroplane and were immediately surrounded by German infantry. A minute or two later, an enemy aeroplane landed beside mine and the German pilot got out. He saluted me. He had a rough field dressing put on my observer's wounds and then he removed a picture of a young lady that I had framed among the instruments in the front seat of the DH 4 and placed it in my pocket.'

The Americans were soon carted off to a German field hospital. Cooper survived third-degree burns on his right arm, captivity and other adventures to become a film director in the 1930s (he was responsible for the motion picture classic *King Kong*).

In all, three crews of the 20th Aero Squadron were killed, two more were captured and the patrol leader returned with a dead observer. When the *Jasta* 12 pilots found out that the ten bombers they had downed only nine days apart all came from the same bombardment group, they were stunned. They realised that 'only the Americans could absorb, or sustain, such losses'.

Ltn d R Alfred Greven strikes a
confident pose with his SSW D III of
Jasta 12. The dark blue fuselage and
white nose is evident, although the
latter appears as off-white because
of stains or poorly applied paint. The
spinner has been removed due to
engine cooling difficulties, although
the previous line-up photo shows it
in place. Note the manufacturer's
'Wotan' transfers on the four-bladed
propeller. Greven's personal insignia
was the white lightning bolt, which
appeared on at least two D VIIs he
flew as well. Greven survived the
war with four victories, all of them
attained with the Fokker D VII
(*A Imrie*)

Another victim of JG II on 26
September was SPAD XIII 4505 from
the 94th Aero Sqaudron flown by 1Lt
Alan Nutt, who fell near Charpentry
(this photo was taken two days
later). Nutt was killed in combat with
Jasta 13, and most likely was one of
Franz Büchner's record four victories
that day. Nutt had only joined
Rickenbacker's 94th 'hat-in-the-ring'
squadron ten days earlier
(*C Woolley via A D Toelle*)

The Yanks took even more casualties on 26 September, for Franz
Büchner had had his greatest single day – he sent down four American
SPADs (and claimed one more that was not allowed). At least one of these
was from the 94th Aero Squadron, and another was the 27th Aero
Squadron machine of Frank Luke's second wingman, 2Lt Ivan Roberts,
who was taken prisoner. Büchner's fellow *Jasta* 13 ace Albert Haussmann
added another Yank SPAD. The dependable *Jasta* 15 veterans contributed
four more fighters from the 13th and 139th Aero Squadrons to make a
total of 14 aircraft subtracted from American forces on the first day of the
Meuse-Argonne offensive.

The only *Staffel* scoreless on the 26th was *Jasta* 19, but the following day
Ltn Hans Körner remedied that deficiency with a SPAD for his fourth
claim. However, the same unit's neophyte pilot Ltn d R Steiling collided
with another aircraft on take-off and was sent to hospital with arm and head
injuries. Two days later victories came to von Beaulieu (his 21st),
Niethammer (4th) and the indomitable Büchner (his 37th, and still no
'Blue Max').

On the evening of 28 September JG II was ordered to relocate to the
5. *Armee* to participate more fully in the battle, which had degenerated
into a bloody struggle deep in the tangled thickets of the Argonne forest.
Jagdstaffeln 15, 19 and the staff would be based at Stenay, and *Staffeln* 12

and 13 moved a bit further south to Charmois. The aircraft were flown over to their new airfields, while 16 lorries transported the rest of the personnel and equipment. On the 29th *Jasta* 19 attacked the SPAD of 2Lt G Woodward of the 95th Aero Squadron just after he had burned a balloon, and Rienau shot him down. Woodward was badly injured and wound up in the same PoW hospital as Merian C Cooper.

With JG II settled in at their new fields, von Boenigk left on a four-week leave. Josef Veltjens, just returned from a leave himself, assumed acting command of JG II, while Hugo Schäfer took over *Jasta* 15. As the group's incredible month drew to a close, von Boenigk looked back at the reasons for their success. He put his finger on it precisely when he wrote:

'The enemy aerial forces there consisted solely of Americans, who were not battle weary as of yet. They had excellent human and aircraft material. When we were nevertheless able to score such exceptional successes, it was almost exclusively a matter of experience. We German pilots had years of experience and, although the Americans flew very courageously and skillfully, we were far superior in battle and combat experience.'

Von Boenigk nevertheless missed, or omitted, the vital fact. For all their success the Germans had usually been unable to prevent the enemy formations from carrying out their missions, and they had little real effect on the outcome of the battles raging beneath them.

Two Fokker D VIIs of *Jasta* 13 illustrate the personal emblems of Werner Niethammer (right) and Ltn d R Grimm (at left, marked with a 'G'). Niethammer's D VII was an OAW-built example, and bore his usual white hammer marking. Grimm's machine is thought to be an earlier Fokker-built D VII. Both pilots contributed to the success of the *Staffel* in September, each despatching two victims during the month

Ltn d R Hugo Schäfer was a crucial member of the small, but deadly, core of *Jasta* 15 pilots who achieved so many successes in the summer and autumn of 1918. Here, he is seated in his earlier *Jasta* 18 Albatros D V marked with his serpent emblem – it is believed that similar insignia adorned his *Jasta* 15 SSW D III and Fokker D VII fighters. Schäfer scored three of his 11 victories in September, including one of three de Havillands from No 104 Sqn credited to his *Staffel* on the 15th

BITTER END

On 30 September all the *Jagdstaffeln* of the 5. *Armee* were placed under the control of JG II. This included *Jagdgruppe* 1 (*Staffeln* 8, 62, 68 and 74), as well as *Jagdgruppe Marville* (*Staffeln* 65 and 67). During the day one *Jasta* would always be on patrol, while the others would have *freie Jagd* (free hunting). By 1 October the move of JG II to Stenay and Charmois was complete, but the pilots complained of the terrible condition of the airfields. At Charmois, three aircraft had already suffered crash landings – the field was described as very small, uneven and covered with high thistles, making it 'a matter of art to land without crashing'. The only compensation was the comfortable quarters.

Acting *Kommandeur* Veltjens had missed out on the glory days of September due to his leave, but started making up for lost time on 1 October. He led *Jasta* 15 into an attack on a SPAD formation south-east of Buzancy at 1640 hrs and achieved his 32nd victory. Von Hantelmann claimed another opponent in this fight, and Klaudat nailed his seventh. Franz Büchner destroyed a Salmson from the 1st Aero Squadron for his 38th, but his meteoric scoring streak would stagnate after this. Except for two unconfirmed claims on the 8th, he did not score again for three weeks.

The ever-increasing shortage of fuel was a real concern for the *Geschwader*, and operations were increasingly curtailed as time went on. In spite of this, on 2 October the reliable *Jasta* 19 commander von Beaulieu netted yet another Bréguet 14B2 from the beleaguered 96th Aero Squadron, although on this occasion its crew came from the 11th Aero Squadron. Along with its persecution of the First Day Bombardment

Franz Büchner scored his final victories in this OAW-built D VII, displaying the full panoply of his unit and personal insignia. The orthochromatic film has rendered the blue of the fuselage as a pale shade. The ace's personal markings consisted of the chequerboard band in the green and white colours of his native Saxony and a fierce lion's head beautifully detailed on a dark green oval. The lion is a prominent element of the coat of arms of Büchner's home city of Leipzig. Note the pale rib tapes on the four-colour fabric covering the wings

This time it was Georg von Hantelmann's turn to celebrate his 20th victory in the usual JG II fashion, and the small but stalwart band of *Jasta* 15 hunters posed for what would be one of their last photos together on Charmois aerodrome near Stenay. By most accounts, this took place on 9 October 1918, and von Hantelmann had a double reason to celebrate – he was leaving his teenage years behind, for he turned 20 this day. These pilots are, from left to right, Vfw Gustav Klaudat, Ltn Hilmar Glöcklen, Ltn Joachim von Ziegesar, Ltn d R Josef Veltjens, von Hantelmann, Ltn d R Hugo Schäfer and Vfw Theodor Weischer. Two weeks after this event, Klaudat would be shot down and wounded by Rickenbacker of the 94th Aero Squadron. The D VII seen here may be von Hantelmann's BMW-engined 465/18 in which he claimed his final victim on 4 November, but that cannot be confirmed. Von Hantelmann survived the war, returning to run his family estates that had been in East Prussia, but were now in the newly formed Poland. He later married, but was sadly murdered on his own estates on 7 September 1924, apparently by poachers

Group, the *Geschwader* seemed to harbour a grudge against the 95th. In a virtual repeat of the experience of Woodhard after his successful balloon attack only four days before, on 3 October 1Lt Walter Avery destroyed a 'gasbag' near Dun-sur-Meuse. Five yellow-nosed Fokkers of *Jasta* 19 then attacked the 'balloon killer', and he was shot down by von Beaulieu after a fierce scrap. The SPAD crashed into a German barracks and Avery sustained a badly broken jaw.

On 25 July Avery had downed *Jasta* 72 ace Carl Menckhoff, who was captured. Now Avery entered captivity himself. On the same day Becker of *Jasta* 12 claimed a SPAD of the 95th's sister unit, the 94th Aero Squadron, and another Yank pilot was captured for Becker's 19th success.

On 4 October the second phase of the Meuse-Argonne offensive began as fresh American troops were brought in to renew the attack with increased vigour. On the same day Prince Max von Baden became Germany's final Imperial Chancellor. This mattered little to the determined pilots of JG II, who flew 78 sorties on the 4th. Four aircraft fell to *Jagdstaffeln* 12, 15 and 19, but von Beaulieu had a tough time with a Salmson 2A2. His Fokker was shot up and he received an injury to his eye, forcing him to break off. The injury was not severe and he remained with his *Staffel*.

The next day, *Jasta* 15's Schäfer and Weischer both got SPADs, one of them from the 22nd Aero Squadron. The 5th also saw Prince Max despatch a cable to President Wilson requesting an armistice, although the men at the front knew nothing of this. On the 6th Wilhelm Leusch of *Jasta* 19 took his score to three with a balloon near Cuisy. It was his first victory since mid-June, and the first balloon claimed by JG II in over six weeks.

After a few days of limited enemy aerial activity, 9 October dawned with hazy skies. The JG II war diary recorded that in the afternoon an immense two-seater formation of over 150 aircraft crossed the lines, but only one machine was brought down, by Niethammer of *Jasta* 13. The inability of even JG II to inflict more damage on such a group was indicative of the ever-increasing numerical superiority and improving tactics of the Allies.

That same day Georg von Hantelmann finally turned 20, and commemorated this by shooting down a USAS fighter – according to most counts, it was his 20th victory as well. His two close friends Schäfer and von Beaulieu similarly destroyed American SPADs.

Better weather on the 10th brought out the First Day Bombardment Group in force, making two multi-squadron raids in the area of Dun-sur-Meuse. At midday the 96th and 11th Aero Squadrons struck Villers-devant-Dun on schedule, but 12 DH 4s from the 20th Aero Squadron arrived over the target late and were again hit by Fokkers, apparently from *Jasta* 12. The Americans lost one crew killed and two observers in other machines seriously wounded. Burgeoning ace Vfw Otto Klaiber was credited with two more 20th Aero DH 4s to add to the one he had shot down on 26 September. The steady scorers Becker, von Beaulieu and Haussmann each added SPADs to their own lists.

The 10th was also an extremely exciting day for two *Jasta* 13 airmen. Gefr Arnold Michaelis was a new pilot, having arrived on 23 September. He and the CO's brother, Felix Büchner, made an attack on a lone observation aeroplane at 4000 metres. In making a turn, the inexperienced Michaelis rammed Büchner's Fokker with terrific force. All four of Büchner's safety strap connections broke and he was thrown out of the cockpit and over the upper wing of his D VII by the impact.

In the split second which followed, he thought he was a dead man – when his parachute snapped open with a great shock. He was naturally greatly relieved, only to discover that the shock of the canopy opening had almost torn through his harness belt, 'but for one centimetre'. The metal belt hooks were bent out of shape as well, and Büchner was left hanging onto what was left of his harness straps for dear life on a 20-minute ride to earth. Michaelis, meanwhile, had abandoned his smashed and burning Fokker, jumping at 3500 metres.

He had been struck on the head during the collision with such force that he passed out during his parachute descent. When he came to his senses, he was on the ground barely inside his own lines, and saw two German infantrymen with trench clubs looming over him in a distinctly unfriendly manner. Because of his bulky and charred flying suit, they could not tell his nationality. Michaelis jumped to his feet and through some enthusiastic cursing convinced them he was indeed German. The narrow escapes made by Felix Büchner and Michaelis were vital for JG II, for at this late stage of the war replacements were ever more difficult to come by.

At this time the responsibility for fighter patrols over the 5. *Armee* was divided. There would be two sectors, split by the River Meuse. JG II would provide fighter cover west of the river, together with *Jagdgruppe La Ferté*, which was under the tactical control of the *Geschwader*. On 12 October German chancellor Prince Max, along with his socialist cabinet minister Philipp Scheidemann, cabled President Wilson that Germany accepted Wilson's Fourteen Points. This news depressed and angered the defiant pilots of JG II.

A photo of mediocre quality, this *Jasta* 13 shot nonetheless significantly shows Ltn d R Felix Büchner fourth from right wearing his Heinecke parachute harness shortly before a patrol. His brother, and commander, Franz is third from left, and at extreme right is Werner Niethammer, wearing the modified version of the Heinecke harness with broader leg straps. Felix Büchner put his parachute to good use on 10 October when his D VII collided with another flown by Arnold Michaelis. However, Felix's harness straps nearly failed – one of several incidents which led to the strengthened version seen on Niethammer

This diverse group of *Jasta* 13 personnel obscure most of one of their unit's OAW-built Fokker D VIIs in late 1918. The aircraft seen here provide good examples of the late form of *Jasta* 13's green and white nose markings. The D VII in the foreground bears the name *GRETEL* – a rare instance of a named JG II aeroplane (*Dr V Koos via P Grosz*)

On the 13th low-lying clouds and rain curtailed aerial operations over the Argonne by either side, but the *Geschwader* war diary also noted, 'The answer of the Government to the Wilson note has provided grounds for a desperate mood. Daily, we expect that we will have to swear a new oath to "excellency" Scheidemann, but that will be completely refused.'

Another blow came on 16 October. *Jasta* 13's stalwart 15-victory ace Albert Haussmann died when his Fokker burst into flames due to undetermined causes over German territory. The failure of his parachute heightened the sense of tragedy. He had already experienced one miraculous escape weeks earlier when he was able to land his crippled Fokker after a collision, but on this day his luck ran out. His wingman Werner Niethammer explained:

'It was a day with real flier's weather – low clouds and rain. A telephone call revealed that an encircled infantry regiment at the front was being strongly harassed by enemy fliers. Haussmann and I started immediately, but neither at the indicated spot, nor to the left nor right of it, did we find even one enemy aircraft. Lest we had flown completely in vain, we began to fire into the enemy trenches.

'When Haussmann flew to me after an attack at about 700 metres, I suddenly saw his machine smoking. Right after that he bailed out. His parachute must have gotten damaged during the jump because it didn't open properly, but formed itself into a sort of pear shape. Haussmann broke his neck when striking the ground. His body was recovered by the *Staffel.* It is possible he had been hit from the ground. But it could have just as easily been one of those mysterious cases of spontaneous ignition of the ammunition or fuel which have never been completely cleared up, and which also cost our Uffz Laabs his life.'

The loss of a pilot of the calibre and experience of Haussmann at this stage of the war had a great impact on the entire group, and other setbacks lay ahead.

Jagdstaffeln 12 and 13 were ordered to move from Charmois to Carignan on 17 October by the high command of the 5. *Armee.* An ensuing flurry of activity followed as the orders were obeyed. Although

After *Jasta* **19** *Staffelführer* Oliver von Beaulieu-Marconnay was seriously wounded on 18 October, his place was taken by the veteran pilot Ltn d R Wilhelm Leusch, who had served in the unit since April 1917. This rare photograph, provided through the courtesy of Manfred Thiemeyer, shows Leusch seated on his Fokker D VII (OAW) emblazoned with a white dragon insignia. The placement of the demarcation line between the yellow nose and dark blue fuselage can be seen clearly. Once again, the light-coloured rib tapes stand out against the five-colour printed camouflage fabric on the wings (*courtesy M Thiemeyer*)

there was some haze and fog on the 18th, visibility was good enough for aerial action, which led to tragedy again. *Jasta* 15 took to the skies in their BMW D VIIs, and Veltjens and von Hantelmann were each credited with the destruction of a DH 4 near Grandpré.

Jasta 19, still equipped with Mercedes Fokkers, did not fare as well. *Staffel* commander Oliver *Freiherr* von Beaulieu-Marconnay essayed an attack on a SPAD, when he was himself accidentally fired upon by a German pilot from *Jasta* 74. The 20-year-old *Staffelführer* was badly wounded in the thigh. He just managed to reach his airfield and was rushed to the hospital, bleeding severely. This was another loss JG II could ill afford – acting command of *Jasta* 19 passed to Wilhelm Leusch, a veteran of the unit with three victories.

Despite poor visibility and clouds, the *Geschwader* made 26 front flights on 21 October. Franz Büchner finally entered the scoring column again with an opponent downed over the Argonne for his 39th. On the same day Georg von Hantelmann was belatedly awarded his 'Hohenzollern', and celebrated by destroying a French SPAD from SPA 159. *Jasta* 12 assisted the beleaguered German infantry by strafing the enemy's positions on the heights east of Cunel, flying at altitudes between 500 and 1000 metres.

22 October was somewhat a repeat of the previous day, with Büchner notching up his 40th victory with a two-seater, while his *Jasta* 13 comrade Niethammer downed another in flames for his sixth. These were the final claims for each pilot, and were in fact the last successes obtained by *Jasta* 13, bringing the unit's total to 123 (according to the war diary).

Meanwhile, six Fokkers from *Jasta* 15 tackled seven SPADs from the 94th 'Hat-in-the-Ring' Aero Squadron over Brieulles at 1700 hrs, and von Hantelmann brought down Lt Raymond Saunders.

Franz Büchner and Josef Veltjens would soon leave the front to attend the final fighter competition at Adlershof, and their scoring runs were at an end – even in these perilous days, it was considered vital for the best operational pilots to test and evaluate the next generation of fighter aircraft. Acting command of JG II passed to Oblt a D Krapfenbauer from 25 October to 2 November.

Having lost Lt Saunders to *Jasta* 15 on 22 October, 94th Aero Squadron commander Capt E V Rickenbacker managed to obtain unknowing revenge on Wednesday. He took off on a lone patrol, hoping to attack a balloon north of Montfaucon. Instead, he saw an Allied balloon torched by a Fokker, which he pursued, only to be jumped by *Jasta* 15 at an altitude of 600 metres. In his colourful book *Fighting the Flying Circus,* Rickenbacker wrote:

'I escaped assassination by four red-nosed Fokkers by the narrowest margin ever vouchsafed to a pilot. One glimpse of the skilful contortions of these Fokkers showed me that I was in for the fight of my life.'

His combat report gives the most reliable version:

'Saw the Fokker who attacked the balloon headed for the enemy lines. Started to cut him off, and while watching him ran into four Fokkers, probably his protection. Fired about 100 rounds into one of them at close range. This took place at about 1655 hrs in the region of Le Grande Carre Ferme. When last seen, the Fokker was in a steep nose-dive. I was unable to follow him further as the three others began firing on me.'

Rickenbacker had ended the career of the six-victory NCO pilot Gustav Klaudat, who managed to return home despite a bullet wound to his left upper arm bone. Klaudat was a modest, but popular, East Prussian whose absence further eroded the combat effectiveness of the *Geschwader.*

On 26 October *Jasta* 19 leader Leusch destroyed a SPAD from the 147th Aero Squadron, but there was little celebration at JG II that evening. The group received the depressing news that Oliver *Freiherr* von Beaulieu-Marconnay had died of his wounds after lingering for ten days. When the Kaiser had been informed the ace was close to death, he had hurriedly signed the document awarding the 20-year-old the highest Prussian tribute, the *Pour le Mérite* (which was not given posthumously). The news arrived six hours after von Beaulieu's death.

Ltn d R Max Kliefoth, a two-month member of *Jasta* 19 with three victories, had been having a bad month in October. On the 2nd he collided with another pilot, getting slightly injured and wrecking two valuable Fokkers. After three weeks he had recovered, but wrecked another D VII in a crash landing on the 25th, emerging unhurt. On the 27th he was permanently removed from the *Staffel* roster, and again Rickenbacker of the 94th Aero Squadron was responsible.

Franz Büchner was able to pose with his wreath-bedecked D VII one final time after scoring for the 40th time on 22 October. It was his last victory, and he was the only JG II pilot besides Berthold to reach this momentous figure. He may have felt a bit hurt that, even with this great accomplishment, he as yet did not wear the *Pour le Mérite,* but that injustice would soon be remedied

Brand new examples of the SSW D IV were still being delivered to JG II at the end of October 1918, but it was a case of too little, too late. This is thought to be D IV 3083/18, which together with its sister aircraft 3082/18 was sent to the *Geschwader* on 25 October. The aircraft saw little, if any, combat service (*P M Grosz*)

In a familiar scenario, bombers of the First Day Bombardment Group were attacked by JG II and other units, and casualties had been sustained. Kliefoth was in pursuit of a crippled DH 4 straggler when Rickenbacker spotted him. The 94th Aero Squadron ace's combat report provides a succinct account:

'Engaged one Fokker firing at one of our bombers. Fired about 200 rounds and noticed his motor stop. I ceased firing and then started manoeuvring him into our lines, but before he landed another SPAD tried to shoot him down. I placed myself between the two and the Fokker landed safely in the region of the southern edge of Bois de Money, turning up on its nose. He had a blue fuselage with white circles on it, and the usual crosses on the wings. Altitude 3000 metres to the ground.'

Kliefoth was captured, as was his intact D VII (despite the vividly exaggerated account of its destruction in Rickenbacker's book). The report of his interrogation reveals he gave both truthful and false information to his captors. He described the markings of his own *Staffel* accurately (after all, they had his D VII to examine) as a yellow nose and blue fuselage, but lied wildly about the colours of the other three units in JG II. He claimed that *Jasta* 19 had 14 aircraft with five spares, and that JG II would soon be getting more BMW Fokkers. He also described the Siemens fighters in detail, and gave particulars of von Beaulieu's death.

The frontline *Jasta* pilots knew relatively little of the disintegrating conditions in the homeland, but the writing was on the wall for those willing to see it. The *Jagdflieger* had enough of their own problems, with shortages of fuel, oil and high-compression engines, and the overwhelming numerical advantage of their opponents. On 25 October the JG II personnel may have been cheered by the news that Oblt von Boenigk and Ltn Franz Büchner had been awarded the *Pour le Mérite* – it was long overdue for the leader of *Jasta* 13. Both men were then in Berlin at the fighter trials, along with Veltjens. They were fortunate, for in just two weeks such awards from the Kaiser would no longer be forthcoming.

With the German forces in retreat, yet another move would soon be forced on JG II, and superfluous supplies and luggage had already been

It is well documented that Hugo Schäfer of *Jasta* 15 flew aeroplanes decorated with a white snake emblem. Photos of this Fokker in American hands, marked with a fanciful winged snake-like creature, have long been assumed by this author and others to show Schäfer's D VII during post-war internment (see Osprey *Aircraft of the Aces* 53). However, evidence provided by respected historian M Thiemeyer has shown that this is Max Kliefoth's D VII after he was shot down and captured by Capt E V Rickenbacker, and it therefore bears the *Jasta* 19 yellow nose. Rickenbacker's combat report stated only that (from his viewpoint) Kliefoth's machine had a blue fuselage 'with white circles', which could be a reasonable distant impression of the serpentine insignia. The report further states that the D VII 'landed safely, turning up on its nose'. During his interrogation by Allied intelligence, Kliefoth correctly described the colours of *Jasta* 19 as a yellow nose and blue fuselage, as evidenced by his own machine

moved back to Carignan in preparation. After the loss of von Beaulieu, Klaudat, and Haussmann, it fell to the remaining veterans of the *Geschwader* to respond to the increased enemy aerial activity on the 29th.

In the morning, a formation of five Salmson 2A2 two-seaters from the 12th Aero Squadron crossed the lines near Champigneulle, with four of them acting as escort for one photography aircraft. This tactic served little purpose when they were bounced by seven Fokkers, flown by pilots the Americans recognised as very skilled. They were from *Jasta* 15, and von Ziegesar would finally gain his third confirmed victim by bringing down the Salmson of Lt Robert Patterson and his unfortunate pilot, Sidney Beauclerk. Patterson barely survived the ordeal, and sat out what was left of the war as a prisoner. In 1963 he wrote this account:

'A dark blue Fokker got under us and killed Lt Beauclerk with a burst of about six shots. The Salmson went into a steep dive and then broke into a tight spiral. As soon as I was able to regain my feet, I looked over toward the pilot and saw him slumped forward. I unbuckled my belt and had started to climb over the pilot's cockpit when I was hit across the head with a bullet. The centrifugal force of the spiral must have sucked me back into the cockpit, because the next thing I knew I was sitting up surrounded by five big Prussian guards, with American shells bursting about 50 yards back of us in a small field. About 20 yards in front of me was the aeroplane, all smashed up. My head and face were bandaged up in good shape.'

In the afternoon of the same day the First Day Bombardment Group made a mass raid on Damvillers, and the trailing 96th Aero Squadron caught the brunt of a concentrated attack. Vfw Richard Schneider of *Jasta* 19 successfully attacked a Bréguet for his third claim – possibly the machine of Lts Stanley and Folger, both of whom were wounded, but made it safely back across the lines.

Even as the Central Powers began to crumble, the *Geschwader* airmen carried on, *Jasta* 12 in particular filling the gap left by absent leaders. As Turkey sued for peace on 30 October, von Hantelmann of *Jasta* 15 achieved his final double. These two are generally credited as raising his score to 25 – he was mentioned in the *Heeresbericht* (Army communiqué) this day. *Staffel* 12 novice Vfw Wittchen bagged a 'SPAD two-seater' at 1030 hrs, which was followed by two more of the same type claimed by his CO Becker (his 22nd) and Vfw Klaiber around noon.

At about 1630 hrs, Becker led *Jasta* 12 into a scrap with a flight of six SPADs from the 22nd Aero Squadron that had been escorting some Bréguets. The 22nd's history states, 'The Germans were good performers, and not to be separated.' The Americans lost two six-victory aces killed in this fight, 1Lts R deB Vernam and J D Beane. They were claimed by Klaiber for his fifth and Ltn Bertling for his initial victory.

Although a desperately poor shot, this view reveals further details of the winged serpentine creature on Kliefoth's Fokker-built D VII, here surrounded by curious American troops. The same insignia appeared on top of the fuselage, but without the wings. Kliefoth had wrecked one D VII in a collision on 2 October, and crashed another just two days before he was shot down. It is this writer's belief that he may have been flying an old Fokker-built D VII from *Jasta* 15 when he was captured on the 27th, re-painted in his unit's yellow-nose markings (*Jasta* 15 had mostly Fokker-built D VIIs, while most other *Jasta* 19 machines were OAW products). It is just possible that the D VII pictured here *had* been formerly flown by Schäfer of *Jasta* 15, but was then turned over to *Jasta* 19 and given a yellow nose and the embellishment of wings and fins on the serpent marking

115

The next day a second SPAD fell to Bertling, and Greven got another, making it seven victories in two days for *Jasta* 12.

FINAL MOVES

On 1 November orders arrived to move the *Geschwader* staff and *Staffeln* 15 and 19 to Carignan. Only a few machines could be flown to the new airfield through the mist before thick fog shut down operations entirely by the afternoon. Although the airfield itself was in decent shape, the billets in Carignan were reported as very poor, with the groundcrew of the two *Jagdstaffeln* quartered in the local cinema.

Even at this late date, 'firsts' were still being achieved as pilots struggled to earn some laurels before hostilities ceased. 3 November (the day Austria-Hungary signed an armistice) was the last great day for the *Geschwader*, with eight victories credited. It might have briefly seemed like the glory days of September had returned, but this was illusory. For one last time, Becker led the white-nosed D VIIs of *Jasta* 12 against a flight of SPADs at 1620 hrs. Ltn Telge and Flgr Rossbach both gained their first – and only – victories, and Bertling, Greven and Wittchen all added to their tallies. Becker also achieved his 23rd victory (the 150th for his *Staffel*), having been proposed for the 'Blue Max' only the day before. By this time, though, the Prussian Order Chancellery had little time or inclination to process such nominations, and Becker never received the order. At about the same time Leusch and Körner of *Jasta* 19 each bagged their final opponents.

The next day Georg von Hantelmann gained the last victory for *Jasta* 15, flying his BMW-engined Fokker D VII 465/18. It was noted as his 26th in his combat report (some historians give him 28). By this late date there was little concern over niceties of detail, and his description of the fight was laconic indeed. 'At 1135 midday, I attacked, near Le Chesne, a single-seater aircraft and shot it down. The adversary was smashed to pieces in falling down.' Eyewitness reports by Ltn Siebert and Vfw Weischer describe von Hantelmann's victim as a SPAD. Like Becker, von Hantelmann would be unsuccessfully nominated for the *Pour le Mérite*.

Indulging in a bit of horseplay for the camera, three *Jasta* 12 mechanics dressed as pilots pose with an OAW-built D VII of their *Staffel* late in 1918. This photo was given to Alex Imrie by the tallest mechanic on the right, surnamed Otto, and *Jasta* 12 pilot Alfred Greven confirmed that these three were indeed enlisted ground personnel. This D VII (OAW) is from a later production batch, and was fitted with more extensive cowling panels, thus the display of white on the nose was also greater. The pilot's personal marking was a black-bordered white fuselage band, barely visible behind the two figures on the left, and an unusual white border was applied to the tailplane and elevators. Once again the fuselage cross is slightly discernible through the dark blue paint, and a tall windscreen and rear-view mirror are fitted (*A Imrie*)

With the situation at the front worsening, the *Kofl* had ordered an urgent move to the auxiliary airfield at Florenville. The transfer commenced on 3 November, but again the shortage of lorries caused delay, worsened by the rain that deteriorated the state of the roads already jammed with retreating troops. The move took several days to complete.

The last successful combat of JG II took place on 6 November at 1625 hrs. *Jasta* 19 commander Wilhelm Leusch led a flight of D VIIs in a dive onto two SPADs that were attacking a two-seater. The Americans were from JG II's traditional foes, the 95th Aero Squadron, piloted by Lt J Pegues and Lt W Vail.

Pegues was too intent on attacking the two-seater to notice the Fokkers, so young Bill Vail pulled up straight into the diving formation to divert them from his wingman. Divert them he did, and found himself in a desperate battle against the whole group. Vail put up an incredibly courageous fight until one accurate burst from Vfw Richard Schneider disabled his engine and another nearly severed his left leg. Operating his rudder bar with his right leg only, Vail struggled to avoid the continuous fire of the pursuing Fokkers as he fell toward the muddy earth of the Argonne with a dead engine – he was credited to Schneider. Vail's SPAD crashed and turned over, pinning the crippled pilot in the mud. American infantry rescued him and he survived after surgeons amputated his leg, bandaged his fractured skull and took a bullet from his arm.

Pegues, meanwhile, was chased across the Meuse by *Jasta* 19 and claimed by Leusch, but he escaped and the claim went unconfirmed. Schneider's fourth victory was thus the last for JG II. Vail was recommended for the Medal of Honour, but like some of his German counterparts, failed to receive his country's highest award.

There were no front flights on 7 November, but the war diary recorded:

'The news came over the radio that negotiators for an armistice had gone to the enemy headquarters. At the same time, alarming reports about the (Allied) demands arrived, but for the time being we cannot believe them.'

Even the legendary fighting spirit of the *Geschwader* began to ebb, as recorded the next day:

'The soldiers' morale deteriorates constantly. Very exaggerated reports from home especially contributed to this. In Germany it seems that

At some point Wilhelm Leusch's *Jasta* 19 Fokker D VII (OAW) fell into French hands, either post-war or after being handed off to some other pilot. Somehow, this photo of the aircraft turned up in the album of French ace Fernand Chavannes of SPA 112, where it proved a red herring for this writer. Chavannes' album implied that this was one of his victims, and because of that, this author and others have attributed it as a possible *Jasta* 66 machine. Obviously, this is now known to be mistaken – how the photo came into Chavannes' possession remains unknown. At any rate, it provides a full view of Leusch's lovely dragon insignia, and reveals the fuselage cross showing up through the blue overpaint (*via P Kilduff*)

The final victory of *Jagdgeschwader* II. On 6 November 1918, Richard Schneider and others of *Jasta* 19 engaged in an unequal contest against two SPADs from the 95th Aero Squadron. Lt 'Bill' Vail took on the entire group of Fokkers to save his wingman, only to be horribly wounded by Schneider. Vail later wrote, 'The Boche shut off my engine with their machine gun fire, then shot off my left leg. I operated the aeroplane with one foot – my right on the rudder bar in the foot clip with which I could pull back for left rudder since my left foot was gone.' Vail's aircraft came down inside American lines and turned over upon impact. This view shows the shattered SPAD after it had been turned right side up by American soldiers as they rescued their badly wounded countryman, who incredibly survived

In a sorry postscript to its wartime career, the forlorn fuselage of Franz Büchner's D VII (OAW) turned up in the hands of the American 138th Aero Squadron at Lay St Rémy in March 1919

soldiers' and workers' councils are being formed. It also seems that a dirty mess has occurred in the Navy (the sailors of the Imperial Navy had mutinied at Kiel on 3 November).'

The *Geschwader* did not fly at all on the 8th, and a mere three front flights on the 9th brought the group's offensive operations to an end with a whimper. That afternoon the *Kofl* of the 5. *Armee* gave orders for the removal of all important equipment by road to the railway station at Trier. Each of the four *Staffeln* sent two lorries with an officer and a squad of guards to ensure their arrival through the disintegrating military situation. On the 10th the reserve aircraft were flown to Trier as well – pilots were to return by ground transport. That afternoon the lorries returned from Trier, and the officer in charge reported on the miserable situation in the hinterlands.

On 11 November 1918 the Armistice went into effect, and the greatest war the world had yet seen ended. In automobiles and trucks, the groundcrews, pilots and other personnel began the long, slow and frustrating journey homeward. On 13 November Ltn Gröbler led 80 men on the start of an ignominious march homeward on foot. After many misadventures and conflicts with Bolshevik-inspired soldiers' and workers' councils, the remnants of the *Geschwader* assembled at Halle an

Groundcrew of the 138th Aero Squadron cut the lion's head insignia from Büchner's D VII, and it is shown with Sgt Walter W Wood at right. Wood brought this historic fabric piece back to the US and donated it to the Army Aeronautical Museum at Wright Field in 1934, but it was sadly destroyed or lost in the 1940s

Jagdgeschwader II epilogue. For many pilots of JG II, the fighting halted only temporarily on 11 November 1918. The post-war political strife within Germany, and disputes on its borders, drew many of the airmen into various *Freikorps* units, and several that survived the Great War met untimely ends within a few years. The *Freikorps* formation seen here is *Freiwillige* Fl. Abt. 418, part of *Grenschutz Ost*, the military command responsible for the defence of Germany's eastern boundary. It was established in December 1918, stationed in Glogau, Silesia, and it drew many former JG II comrades into its ranks. From left to right in the front row, fourth is Werner Niethammer, fifth is Hermann Becker, sixth is Oskar von Boenigk and eighth is Wilhelm Leusch. In the back row, at extreme left is Rudolf Rienau, and seventh from left (to the right of Leusch) is Fritz Gewert

der Salle to be officially demobilised on 23 November 1918, and JG II passed into history.

Close to the conflict's end, record keeping and the victory confirmation process suffered due to the attendant chaos, and it is difficult to come up with an undisputed number of victories for JG II. One authority places the JG II total at 339, another gives the unit 348 victories. The *Geschwader* lost 18 men killed in action or from mortal wounds, with another four lost to fatal crashes. In addition, the group had eight pilots taken prisoner and another eight wounded in action or injured in accidents, for a total of 38 casualties.

For many of those who survived the fighting was not over, and a notable percentage met untimely ends in the post-war civil chaos that engulfed Germany, or from tragic accidents and illness. The war took its toll in more ways than one.

APPENDICES

APPENDIX 1

JAGDGESCHWADER Nr II COMMANDERS

Commander	Dates of Command	Notes
Hptm Adolf Ritter von Tutschek	2/2/18 to 15/3/18	KIA 15/3/18
Hptm Rudolf Berthold	18/3/18 to 10/8/18	WIA 10/8/18
Hptm Hugo Weingarth	10/8/18 to 12/8/18	stv*
Rittm Heinz Anton von Brederlow	12/8/18 to 12/8/18	to JgGrp 11
Hptm Rudolf Berthold	12/8/18 to 13/8/18	to hospital
Ltn d R Josef Veltjens	13/8/18 to 31/8/18	stv
Oblt Oskar Frhr von Boenigk	31/8/18 to 28/9/18	leave
Ltn d R Josef Veltjens	28/9/18 to 12/10/18	stv
Oblt Oskar Frhr von Boenigk	12/10/18 to 25/10/18	leave
Oblt a D Fritz Krapfenbauer	25/10/18 to 2/11/18	stv
Oblt Oskar Frhr von Boenigk	2/11/18 to 11/11/18	died 30/1/46 in Soviet captivity

* Those who were temporary acting commanders are noted as stv (stellvertreter)

APPENDIX 2

JAGDGESCHWADER Nr II *JASTA* COMMANDERS

Commander	Dates of Command	Notes
Jasta 12		
Oblt Paul Blumenbach	2/2/18 to 18/5/18	to *Jasta* 31
Ltn Robert Hildebrandt	18/5/18 to 13/7/18	to *Jasta* 69
Ltn d R Hermann Becker	13/7/18 to 11/11/18	to end of war
Jasta 13		
Ltn d R Wolfgang Güttler	2/2/18 to 20/2/18	killed in crash
Oblt Alex Thomas	21/2/18 to 1/5/18	to *Jasta* 69
Ltn d R Wilhelm Schwartz	1/5/18 to 15/6/18	WIA
Ltn Franz Büchner	15/6/18 to 11/11/18	to end of war
Jasta 15		
Ltn Hans Hermann von Budde	2/2/18 to 14/3/18	to *Idflieg*
Ltn d R August Raben	14/3/18 to 20/3/18	to *Jasta* 18
Oblt Ernst Wilhelm Turck	20/3/18 to 18/5/18	to *Jasta* 54
Ltn d R Josef Veltjens	18/5/18 to 13/8/18	to JG II as CO, stv
Ltn Joachim von Ziegesar	13/8/18 to 18/8/18	stv
Ltn d R Hugo Schäfer	18/8/18 to 12/10/18	stv
Ltn d R Josef Veltjens	12/10/18 to 11/11/18	to end of war

Commander	Dates of Command	Notes
Jasta 19		
Ltn Konrad von Bülow-Bothkamp	2/2/18 to 14/2/18	posted due to brother's death
Ltn d R Walter Göttsch	14/2/18 to 10/4/18	KIA
Ltn d R Arthur Rahn	10/4/18 to 18/4/18	stv
Ltn d L Hans Pippart	18/4/18 to 20/5/18	leave
Ltn d R Gerlt	20/5/18 to 11/6/18	stv
Ltn d L Hans Pippart	11/6/18 to 11/8/18	KIA
Ltn d R Gerlt	11/8/18 to 12/8/18	stv
Ltn d R Ulrich Neckel	12/8/18 to 1/9/18	to *Jasta* 6
Ltn Oliver von Beaulieu-Marconnay	1/9/18 to 18/10/18	WIA, died 26/10/18
Ltn d R Wilhelm Leusch	18/10/18 to 26/10/18	stv
Ltn d R Wilhelm Leusch	26/10/18 to 11/11/18	to end of war

APPENDIX 3

JAGDGESCHWADER Nr II ACES WHO RECEIVED THE *ORDEN POUR LE MÉRITE*

Recipient	JG II Unit(s)	Date of Award	Total Victories
Hptm Rudolf Berthold*	JG II	12/10/16	44
Oblt Adolf Ritter von Tutschek*	JG II	3/8/17	27
Ltn Kurt Wüsthoff*	*Jasta* 15	22/11/17	27
Ltn d R Josef Veltjens	*Jasta* 15	16/8/18	34/35
Oblt Oskar Frhr von Boenigk	JG II	25/10/18	26/27
Ltn Franz Büchner	*Jasta* 13	25/10/18	40
Ltn Oliver von Beaulieu-Marconnay	*Jasta* 15,19	26/10/18	25/26
Ltn d R Ulrich Neckel*	*Jasta* 12,13,19	8/11/18	30

* Did not receive the *Pour le Mérite* during their service in a JG II unit, but rather before or after they served in JG II

APPENDIX 4

JAGDGESCHWADER Nr II ACES WHO RECEIVED THE KNIGHT'S CROSS WITH SWORDS OF THE ROYAL HOHENZOLLERN HOUSE ORDER

Recipient	JG II Unit(s)	Date of Award	Total Victories
Hptm Rudolf Berthold*	JG II	27/8/16	44
Hptm Adolf Ritter von Tutschek*	JG II	11/7/17	27
Ltn d R Walter Göttsch	*Jasta* 19	23/8/17	20
Ltn d L Hans Pippart	*Jasta* 13,19	2/5/18	22
Ltn d R Hermann Becker	*Jasta* 12	15/5/18	23
Ltn d R Josef Veltjens	*Jasta* 15	20/5/18	34/35
Ltn d R Arthur Rahn	*Jasta* 15,19	1/8/18	6
Hptm Oskar Frhr von Boenigk*	JG II	14/8/18	26/27
Ltn Franz Büchner	*Jasta* 13	20/8/18	40
Ltn Georg von Hantelmann	*Jasta* 15	21/10/18	26/28

* Received the Order before their service with JG II

APPENDIX 4

NOTES ON SELECTED *JAGDGESCHWADER* Nr II AIRCRAFT SERIAL NUMBERS

Aircraft	Pilot (if known)	Details
***Jagdstaffel* 12**		
Albatros D V 2194/17	*Hptm* Adolf von Tutschek	13 and 23/2/18
Fokker Dr I 216/17	*Hptm* Adolf von Tutschek	19/2/18
Fokker Dr I 217/17	*Oblt* Paul Blumenbach	March 1918
Fokker Dr I 436/17	*Ltn* Hoffmann, *Ltn* Greven	March–June 1918
Fokker Dr I 404/17	*Hptm* Adolf von Tutschek	February–March 1918
Halberstadt CL II 14251/17		hack aircraft
SSW D IV 7553/17		July 1918
***Jagdstaffel* 13**		
Fokker Dr I 193/17	*Ltn d R* Wilhelm Schwartz	15/5/8
Fokker D VII 373/18	*Uffz* Heinrich Piel	June 1918
***Jagdstaffel* 15**		
Fokker Dr I 412/17	*Ltn* Claus von Waldow	March 1918, 'N'
Fokker Dr I 401/17	*Ltn d R* Kurt Monnington	March 1918
Fokker Dr I 218/17	*Ltn* Bergner	March 1918
Fokker D VII 382/18	*Ltn* Georg von Hantelmann	Wüsthoff PoW 7/6/18
Fokker D VII F 465/18	*Ltn* Georg von Hantelmann	4/11/18
***Jagdstaffel* 19**		
Albatros D V 2104/17	*Uffz* Albert Tybelsky	circa November 1917
Fokker Dr I 202/17	*Ltn d R* Walter Göttsch	February 1918, '2'
Fokker Dr I 167/17		February 1918, '3'
Fokker Dr I 417/17		April 1918
Fokker Dr I 419/17	*Ltn d R* Walter Göttsch	KIA 10/4/18
SSW D III 8346/17	Prepared for Göttsch but not flown	April 1918
SSW D III 8342/17		April 1918
Fokker Dr I 433/17	*Ltn d R* Arthur Rahn	April 1918
Fokker Dr I 503/17	*Ltn* Hans Körner	April 1918
Fokker Dr I 504/17	*Ltn d R* Rudolf Rienau	April 1918
Fokker Dr I 471/17	*Ltn d L* Hans Pippart	circa May 1918
Fokker D VII 258/18	*Ltn d R* Rudolf Rienau	May/June 1918
Fokker E V 107/18	*Ltn* Ernst Riedel	Killed in accident 16/8/18

COLOUR PLATES

All of the art in this section has been created by artist and World War 1 aficionado Harry Dempsey, who worked patiently and tirelessly with the author to illustrate the aeroplanes as accurately as circumstances will permit. The colours portrayed are approximations only. The multitude of Fokker D VII cowling details, national insignia variations and lozenge fabric applications make those aircraft particularly hazardous to define. The pioneering research and assistance of Alex Imrie was – as always – of tremendous value. Respected historian Manfred Thiemeyer also provided a great deal of vital information, insights and rare photographic data. The author is also indebted to the assistance rendered by Dan-San Abbott, Helge K – Werner Dittmann, Rick Duiven, Peter Kilduff, Paul S Leaman, Jörn Leckscheid, Dr Glen K Merrill, Terry 'Taz' Phillips, Ray Rimell, Dave Roberts and others too numerous to name.

1

Albatros D V D.2014/17 of Uffz Albert Tybelsky, *Jasta* 19, St Loup, late summer 1917

Tybelsky's D V illustrates the standard form of white 'shadow-shaded' black initial favoured by *Jasta* 19 for personal identification. The aircraft was apparently otherwise in factory finish, with green and mauve camouflaged wings and tailplane. The rudders of *Jasta* 19 D Vs at St Loup were uniformly dark, which has been interpreted here as camouflage green.

2

Pfalz D III (serial unknown) of Ltn Claus von Waldow, *Jasta* 15, La Neuville, autumn 1917

The date and location of the photo on which this profile is based is unconfirmed, but this Pfalz was clearly flown by von Waldow. *Jasta* 15 had no known unit marking in this period. The colours of the red and white bands are also speculative, but this machine otherwise bore the usual *silbergrau* finish.

3

Pfalz D III 4184/17 of Vfw Hegeler, *Jasta* 15, Autremencourt, 26 February 1918

Hegeler was shot down and made a PoW on 26 February in this aircraft, which was given the captured aircraft number G141. It had Mercedes engine number 35482 and an Axial propeller. The rudder was later painted brown and marked with a British roundel. The original descriptions state clearly that the fuselage band was black.

4

Albatros D V (serial unknown) of Vfw Ulrich Neckel, *Jasta* 12, Toulis, March 1918

The official *Kogenluft* photographer visited Toulis on 15 March 1918 and recorded the appearance of the Albatros and Fokker fighters of *Jasta* 12 for posterity. This Albatros D V exemplifies the *Staffel* marking practices of the time – black tail and a white spinner ahead of a black cowling band. The black-bordered white chevron was Neckel's personal insignia that was repeated on his Dr I. The wings were probably covered in five-colour fabric.

5

Fokker Dr I 202/17 of Ltn Walter Göttsch, *Jasta* 19, Cuirieux, circa February 1918

Initially some *Staffel* 19 triplanes were marked with large yellow numbers aft of the cockpit as personal insignia. The commander Göttsch flew this Dr I for a short time, and it bore the white cowling and black/yellow tail bands of this *Jasta*. The serial number was obscured by the yellow '2', so this was re-painted in yellow beneath the tailplane.

6

Pfalz D III (serial and pilot unknown), *Jasta* 12, Toulis, March 1918

This is the only Pfalz visible in the familiar line-up photos of *Jasta* 12 at Toulis. It displayed the usual *Staffel* markings in black and white, and a simple black vertical stripe ahead of the fuselage cross sufficed for personal embellishment.

7

Fokker Dr I 404/17 of Hptm Adolf von Tutschek, JG II, Toulis, March 1918

Von Tutschek's Dr I is depicted as it appeared on the day of his death, 15 March 1918. It displayed the stereotypical *Jasta* 12 markings, and the top wing cross fields have been reduced with black paint to leave a narrow white border. The works number 1988 was stencilled on the struts and in the other usual locations. Black and white streamers trailed from both lower wings.

8

Fokker Dr I 217/17 of Oblt Paul Blumenbach, *Jasta* 12, Toulis, March 1918

As *Staffelführer* of *Jasta* 12, Blumenbach flew this triplane in March. It was decorated with crossing white bands on the fuselage sides, which were repeated on top of the fuselage. This Dr I survived for quite some time at *Jasta* 12, and even after Blumenbach had left the unit it still bore his personal insignia. The crosses had gone through several changes and the rudder was painted white by the time it was photographed at Les Mesnil in June.

9

Fokker Dr I 436/17 of Ltn Paul Hoffmann, *Jasta* 12, Toulis, March 1918

Marked with three horizontal white bands as a personal emblem, this Dr I was flown by Hoffmann at this time. On 1 April Hoffmann was severely wounded in the stomach and pelvis. He managed to return to Toulis and land safely, but died the next day. Dr I 436/17 stayed in use at *Jasta* 12 until June, being flown on occasion by Alfred Greven.

10

Fokker Dr I (serial unknown) of Ltn d R Hans Müller, *Jasta* 15, Autremenecourt, March 1918

Future ace Hans Müller flew this Dr I briefly with *Jasta* 15 before the switch with *Jasta* 18 occurred on 20 March. His personal emblem was the black/white striped fuselage band, and this decoration was repeated in chevron style on the tailplane and elevator. In common with triplanes of other units in JG II, the *Jasta* 15 Dr Is all displayed white cowlings.

11

Fokker Dr I 412/17 of Ltn Claus von Waldow, *Jasta* 15, Autremencourt, March 1918

Ltn von Waldow continued to use his enigmatic 'N' insignia, marked in stylised fashion, on his Dr I 412/17. This aircraft certainly bore a white cowling and may later have had its rudder overpainted a dark colour (brown?) as a unit marking, as did other *Jasta* 15 triplanes.

12

Fokker Dr I (serial unknown) of Ltn d L Hans Pippart, *Jasta* 13, Reneuil-Ferme, March 1918

Pippart's aircraft was painted with the *Staffel* 13 unit marking of a white tail section along with the JG II white engine cowling. His personal emblem was the white wavy line on the fuselage.

13

Fokker Dr I 433/17 of Ltn d R Arthur Rahn, *Jasta* 19, Balatre, April 1918

Rahn used a white-bordered band of white diamonds as a personal emblem on his *Jasta* 19 Dr I. The works number 2058 was marked in the usual locations and the serial was re-painted above the rudder cross.

14

Fokker Dr I 429/17 (pilot unknown), *Jasta* 19, Balatre, April 1918

The serial number of this Dr I is tentatively thought to have been 429/17 (works number 2013), based upon close examination of photos. It was marked with an individual emblem of a simple white triangle on the fuselage sides and top. The usual *Jasta* 19 yellow and black tail bands and white cowling were also applied. The serial number was re-painted in small characters on the fuselage side above the white triangle.

15

Fokker Dr I 503/17 of Ltn Hans Körner, *Jasta* 19, Balatre, April 1918

Körner's triplane 503/17 (works number 2130) was personally distinguished with a striking white lightning flash painted on the fuselage top and sides. An Oigee telescopic sight was affixed on tubes bolted to the guns. The upper wing crosses appear to have been backed up by full white fields.

16

Fokker Dr I 504/17 of Ltn d R Rudolf Rienau, *Jasta* 19, Balatre, April 1918

Rienau identified his Dr I with this dazzling diagonal stripe pattern. The top view of this aircraft on page 62 illustrates the treatment of the wing crosses and tailplane unit markings that characterised most *Jasta* 19 triplanes.

17

Fokker Dr I 193/17 of Ltn d R Wilhelm Schwartz, Les Mesnil, May 1918

This aircraft was photographed on 15 May at Quesmy. It certainly seems to have borne the unit colours of a blue fuselage and dark green cowling, ordered by Berthold. The retention of the old iron cross insignia on full white fields is quite unusual for this late date – perhaps this helped to identify the *Staffel* commander's machine? The works

number 1911 appeared in the typical locations, and the wings retained their streaky finish.

18

Albatros D V (serial unknown) of Oblt Paul Wilhelm Turck, *Jasta* 15, Balatre, April 1918

Turck's machine provides a classic example of the 'Berthold colours' as applied to aircraft of *Jasta* 18/15. Based on the colours of Berthold's old infantry regiment dress tunics, these aircraft featured a red nose and the rest of the fuselage and tailplane in a very dark blue. Most of the Albatros and Pfalz fighters had light coloured undersides – probably light blue on the Albatros D Vs. Turck's D V was emblazoned with his own comet design, and had green and mauve camouflaged wings.

19

Pfalz D IIIa (serial unknown) of Ltn Hans Burckhard von Buttlar, *Jasta* 15, Balatre, April 1918

Like the other aircraft photographed at Balatre, this Pfalz had previously seen service in *Jasta* 18, with iron cross insignia that had been changed to early *Balkenkreuz* form. It had earlier been flown by Vfw Hitschler in *Jasta* 18, and von Buttlar had over-painted his insignia with a dark band and added his own hunting horn emblem. This D IIIa had lower wings with the pointed tips of the D III, and uppersurfaces of both wings were painted dark blue. This aircraft was apparently flown without a spinner.

20

Albatros D V (serial unknown) of Ltn d R Josef Veltjens, *Jasta* 15, Balatre, April 1918

The white 'Indian arrow' identified this aircraft as the D V flown by Veltjens, which displayed the usual *Jasta* 18/15 colouration. The wheel covers were a pale colour, probably light blue. The cabane struts were likely red, and the wings were in green/mauve camouflage.

21

Albatros D V (serial unknown) of Ltn Werner Niethammer, Les Mesnil, June 1918

Again the date is approximate for this depiction of Niethammer's Albatros, which displays an early version of the *Jasta* 13 markings as specified by Berthold – green nose and dark blue fuselage. This profile is based on a photo of a wingless fuselage being salvaged, and the absence of wings makes it impossible to determine if this was in fact a D V or D Va – the latter is just as likely. Similarly, the green/mauve wings depicted are an assumption.

22

Siemens-Schuckert Werke D III (serial unknown) of Ltn Joachim von Ziegesar, *Jasta* 15, Les Mesnil, May 1918

This D III is an example of the first group of Siemens fighters tested by JG II in May, and one of the very few for which a photograph survives showing the machine in full unit heraldry. It displayed the *Jasta* 15 markings of a dark blue fuselage and red nose. The blue was applied to the plywood-covered fin and horizontal stabiliser, but the elevator remained in five-colour fabric, as did the wings. The interplane struts appear to have been painted to match the lozenge fabric. The pilot's three white feathers adorned the fuselage.

23
Fokker Dr I (serial unknown) of Ltn Hans Besser, *Jasta* 12, Les Mesnil, June 1918
This long-serving triplane was part of a weathered group photographed in June 1918, shortly before retirement. By this time many of the *Jasta* 12 triplanes had apparently had additional black and white colouration added, which often (as here) extended the length of the fuselage. This aircraft appeared very worn indeed, and displayed black 'N' markings on a faded white band aft of the cockpit. The wings may have been additionally over-painted as well, but they are cautiously depicted as worn factory finish.

24
Fokker D VII (serial unknown) of Hptm Rudolf Berthold, JG II, Les Mesnil, June 1918
Berthold flew, and wrecked, several different D VIIs in his turbulent time at the front, but this is the only one of which a photo has surfaced. When photographed, the fuselage blue had been painted up to the mid-point of the cockpit, and the red was confined to the metal cowling panels, wheels, and possibly struts. Blue décor was also applied to the upper surface of both wings, and a white panel appeared on the upper wing centre section. Berthold's winged sword badge was emblazoned on both sides of the blue fuselage. The undersides of the wings were probably covered in five-colour printed fabric.

25
Fokker D VII 373/18 of Uffz Heinrich Piel, *Jasta* 13, Les Mesnil, June 1918
Piel's machine was an aircraft from the first production batch, and would have left the factory with streaked camouflage on the fuselage. At *Jasta* 13 this was covered with the unit colours, but the white serial number showed through the blue to some degree. Piel's aircraft proves the stork's appeal was not limited to the French. Three cockade-marked bullet hole patches appeared in close proximity to the stork on the port side.

26
Fokker D VII (serial unknown) of Uffz Johannes Fritzche, Les Mesnil, June 1918
The attribution of this aircraft to Fritsche is an assumption based on the 'F' insignia. It appears to be a D VII from the second Fokker production batch with the heavily louvred top cowling. It otherwise displayed typical *Jasta* 13 markings for the period.

27
Siemens-Schuckert Werke D III (serial and pilot unknown), *Jasta* 15, Chéry-les-Pouilly, July 1918
Again, information on this particular aircraft is lacking and the date and location are assumed, but it certainly seems to display *Jasta* 15 unit markings. It was one of those D IIIs that had been modified in accordance to specifications issued by *Idflieg*. The wings were covered in five-colour fabric, and a personal 'V' of unknown significance was displayed.

28
Fokker D VII (OAW) (serial unknown) of Ltn Herbert Bock, *Jasta* 12, Chéry-les-Pouilly, August 1918
Bock was a *Jasta* 12 pilot of long service whose OAW-built D VII provides a good example of *Staffel* markings as applied to the D VIIs. This pilot's personal emblem was a play on words, as the German word for 'ram' is Bock. This emblem was applied over a vertical band of unknown colour – probably a previous marking which has been painted over as shown.

29
Fokker D VII (OAW) (serial unknown) of Ltn d R Hans Besser, *Jasta* 12, Chéry-les-Pouilly, August 1918
Another example of the *Jasta* 12 markings format is this D VII adorned with the white broom emblem of Hans Besser. The wheel covers were marked with the early OAW camouflage colours of purple and green in a hazy application, and four-colour fabric covered the wings.

30
Siemens-Schuckert Werke D III (serial unknown) of Ltn d R Alfred Greven, *Jasta* 12, Chéry-les-Pouilly, August 1918
This was another reconditioned D III, and it displayed Greven's individual symbol of a white lightning bolt on the blue fuselage. The unit distinction consisted of the white nose, which looks almost like natural metal in the photo, but dirty or poorly applied white is more likely. The wings were covered in five-colour fabric, and the wheel covers appear to have been white. The interplane struts were painted in imitation of the printed fabric.

31
Siemens-Schuckert Werke D IV 7553/17 (pilot unknown), *Jasta* 12, Chéry-les-Pouilly, July/August 1918
In its first configuration, this aircraft was fitted with duralumin wing spars and competed in the first fighter competition in January 1918, where it crashed. After conversion to D IV configuration, it was sent to JG II for frontline evaluation in April. 7553/17 was then returned to the factory for modification to the new *Idflieg* standards, and was sent to JG II a second time on 22 July 1918. It is seen in its final version in full *Jasta* 12 warpaint.

32
Fokker D VII (OAW) (pilot and serial unknown) of *Jasta* 12, Giraumont, September 1918
This late aircraft featured a more extensive display of the *Staffel* white nose marking. A black-bordered white band served as personal distinction, along with an unusual white border to the tailplane and elevator – see page 64. Four-colour fabric covered the wings.

33
Fokker D VII (serial unknown) of Ltn d R Grimm, *Jasta* 13, Giraumont, September 1918
The D VII marked with the 'G' insignia of Grimm was an early Fokker-built machine of lengthy service. It illustrates the later form of *Jasta* 13 unit marking – a green nose display of lesser area, bordered by a white band. Many of the details of this illustration are tentative, being based on a small photo of poor quality.

34
Fokker D VII (serial unknown) of Ltn d R Paul Wolff, *Jasta* 13, Tichémont, September 1918
Wolff was shot down and made a PoW in this machine on 14 September. He marked his D VII with a white arrow motif, and photos reveal that the upper cowling on the

starboard side was a lighter colour than the usual dark green applied to the side panel. This may have been a replaced component, and we have chosen to illustrate the starboard side as similar, but this is by no means confirmed. The wheel covers were green as well, and four-colour fabric covered the wings.

35
Fokker D VII (OAW) of Gefr Arnold Michaelis, *Jasta* 13, Carignan, October 1918
Michaelis decorated his OAW-built machine with his initial. As was often the case, the fuselage cross could still be discerned through the blue paint. The wings were covered in four-colour fabric, and this aircraft is thought to have been a BMW-powered machine as well.

36
Fokker D VII (serial unknown) of Ltn Oliver von Beaulieu-Marconnay, *Jasta* 15, Chéry-les-Pouilly, August 1918
This much-modified BMW-engined D VII is thought to have been formerly flown by Berthold, as what seems to be his insignia is visible beneath the pilot's familiar '4D' emblem. It was fitted with an unusual windscreen and modified cowling panels with additional louvres. The uppersurfaces of the wings seem to have been dark blue, which would make sense if it were a former Berthold machine.

37
Fokker D VII (serial unknown) of Ltn Joachim von Ziegesar, *Jasta* 15, Chéry-les-Pouilly, August 1918
Again, much of this depiction is tentative in nature, based as it is on a mediocre photograph. Von Ziegesar's usual three white feathers marked his D VII, which may have displayed red cabane and interplane struts. This was likely a BMW-powered machine.

38
Fokker D VII (serial unknown) of Ltn d R Max Kliefoth, *Jasta* 19, Stenay, October 1918
This attractive, but controversial, D VII was photographed in American hands, and was formerly assumed by the author to have borne the markings of Hugo Schäfer of *Jasta* 15, who certainly did use a serpent emblem. However, new information provided by historian Manfred Thiemeyer indicates that this was the aircraft being flown by Kliefoth of *Jasta* 19 when he was shot down by Rickenbacker on 26 October. Kliefoth's interrogation report confirms that his machine had a yellow nose and blue fuselage (and not a red nose as stated in the exaggerated account in *Fighting the Flying Circus*). Since Kliefoth had just crashed a D VII two days before, and this machine exhibits considerable wear, it is the author's theory that this D VII was a former *Jasta* 15 machine handed down to *Jasta* 19, and the markings may indeed be an altered version of Schäfer's emblem. No doubt this interpretation will stir more debate.

39
Fokker D VII (OAW) (serial unknown) of Ltn d R Wilhelm Leusch, *Jasta* 19, Stenay, October 1918
While this was formerly erroneously assumed to be a *Jasta* 66 machine, there is now *no doubt* that it bears the markings of Wilhelm Leusch, the last commander of *Jasta* 19. The dark blue fuselage served as a background for Leusch's lovely white dragon emblem, which was based on the image in an advertisement for the industrial firm of Unterberg & Helmle. This may have been a BMW-engined D VII, and five-colour fabric covered the wings, with light rib tapes. Thanks go to Manfred Thiemeyer and Jörn Leckscheid for this data.

40
Fokker D VII (OAW) (serial unknown) of Ltn Franz Büchner, *Jasta* 13, Carignan, October 1918
Büchner flew at least three D VIIs, and this was the final BMW-engined one flown at the end of the war. It displayed his complete heraldry, with the chequerboard band in the Saxon green and white colours, along with his famous lion's head marking. The wings were covered in four-colour fabric on top and bottom surfaces.

BIBLIOGRAPHY

BAILEY, FRANK AND CONY, CHRISTOPHE, *The French Air Service War Chronology 1914–1918,* London, 2001

BARTH, CLARENCE G, *History of the 20th Aero Squadron,* Nashville, TN, 1990

DUIVEN, RICK, Das königliche preussische Jagdgeschwader II, Parts 1,2, and 3, *Over the Front,* Volume 9, No. 3 and 4, Volume 10, No 1, 1994–1995

DUIVEN, RICK, FRANKS, NORMAN AND BAILEY, FRANK, *The Jasta War Chronology,* London

FERKO, A E, *Fliegertruppe 1914–1918 No 2,* Salem, OH, 1986

FRANKS, NORMAN, BAILEY, FRANK AND GUEST, RUSSELL, *Above the Lines,* London, 1993

FRANKS, NORMAN, BAILEY, FRANK AND DUIVEN, RICK, *The Jasta Pilots,* London, 1996

GORDON, DENNIS, *The Lafayette Flying Corps, The American Volunteers in the French Air Service in World War One,* Atglen, PA, 2000

GRAY, RANDAL, *Kaiserschlacht 1918 – The Final German Offensive, Osprey Campaign Series No 11,* London, 1991

GROSZ, PETE, *Windsock Datafile 9, Fokker D VII,* Berkhamsted, 1989

GROSZ, PETER, *Windsock Datafile 25, Fokker D VIII,* Berkhamsted, 1991

GROSZ, PETER, *Windsock Datafile 29, SSW D III-D IV,* Berkhamsted, 1991

GROSZ, PETER, AND FERKO, A E, 'The Fokker Dr I –
A Reappraisal', *Air Enthusiast No 8,* London, 1978

HENSHAW, TREVOR, *The Sky Their Battlefield,* London, 1995

IMRIE, ALEX, *The Fokker Triplane,* London, 1992

IMRIE, ALEX, *Osprey Airwar 17 – German Fighter Units
June 1917–1918,* London, 1978

IMRIE, ALEX, *Vintage Warbirds 16: German Army Air Aces
of World War One,* Poole, 1987

KILDUFF, PETER, *Germany's First Air Force,* London, 1991

LANGSDORFF, W (ED), *Flieger am Feind,* Gütersloh, circa
1935

LEAMAN, PAUL, *Fokker Dr I Triplane – A World War One
Legend,* 2003

MILLER, THOMAS G, JR, *History of the First Day
Bombardment Group,* West Roxbury, MA, circa 1965

MÖLLER, HANNS, *Kampf und Sieg eines
Jagdgeschwaders*, Berlin, 1939

O'CONNOR, N, *Aviation Awards of Imperial Germany in
World War I and the Men Who Earned Them,* Vols 1 to VII,
Princeton, NJ and Atglen, PA, 1988 to 2003

RIMELL, RAY (ED), *Fokker D VII Anthology No 1,*
Berkhamsted, 1997

THEILHABER, FELIX A, *Jüdische Flieger im Weltkrieg,*
Berlin, 1924

THOMAS, GERALD C, *The First Team: Thornton D
Hooper and America's First Bombing Squadron,* Dallas,
TX, 1992

WOOLLEY, CHARLES, *First to the Front – The Aerial
Adventures of 1st Lt Waldo Heinrichs and the 95th Aero
Squadron,* Atglen, PA, 1999

WOOLLEY, CHARLES, *The Hat in the Ring Gang – The
Combat History of the 94th Aero Squadron in World War I,*
Atglen, PA, 2001

WOOLLEY, CHARLES, AND CRAWFORD, BILL, *Echoes of
Eagles,* New York, 2003

ZUERL, W, *Pour le Mérite-Flieger,* Munich, 1938

INDEX